THE
NEURODIVERSE
CLASSROOM

by the same author

**A Practical Guide to Happiness in Children
and Teens on the Autism Spectrum**
A Positive Psychology Approach
ISBN 978 1 78592 347 0
eISBN 978 1 78450 681 0

of related interest

101 Inclusive and SEN Maths Lessons
Fun Activities and Lesson Plans for Children Aged 3–11
Claire Brewer and Kate Bradley
ISBN 978 1 78592 101 8
eISBN 978 1 78450 364 2
from the 101 Inclusive and SEN Lessons *series*

Specific Learning Difficulties –
What Teachers Need to Know
Diana Hudson
Illustrated by Jon English
ISBN 978 1 84905 590 1
eISBN 978 1 78450 046 7

The Dyspraxic Learner
Strategies for Success
Alison Patrick
ISBN 978 1 84905 594 9
eISBN 978 1 78450 049 8

Okay Kevin
A Story to Help Children Discover
How Everyone Learns Differently
James Dillon
Illustrated by Kara McHale
ISBN 978 1 78592 732 4
eISBN 978 1 78450 432 8

THE NEURODIVERSE CLASSROOM

A TEACHER'S GUIDE TO INDIVIDUAL LEARNING NEEDS AND HOW TO MEET THEM

Victoria Honeybourne

Jessica Kingsley *Publishers*
London and Philadelphia

First published in 2018
by Jessica Kingsley Publishers
73 Collier Street
London N1 9BE, UK
and
400 Market Street, Suite 400
Philadelphia, PA 19106, USA

www.jkp.com

Library of Congress Cataloging in Publication Data
A CIP catalog record for this book is available from the Library of Congress

British Library Cataloguing in Publication Data
A CIP catalogue record for this book is available from the British Library

ISBN 978 1 78592 362 3
eISBN 978 1 78450 703 9

Printed and bound in Great Britain

NOTE FROM THE AUTHOR

Developing and growing in one aspect of your life often has a knock-on effect on other parts of your life, and that has been particularly true for me over the past decade.

Receiving a diagnosis of Asperger syndrome in my 20s was pivotal for me – allowing me to gain deeper awareness, understanding and self-acceptance. This also influenced my professional life as a teacher and I decided to specialise in supporting students who had similar differences to myself.

Since then, however, my thinking has developed further. I have come to realise that being different is, in fact, very normal indeed; many of the difficulties 'different' individuals encounter are created simply by other people's attitudes and by living in a society which has been designed for just one way of being.

In this book I want to offer a different way of viewing neurological differences in schools. Rather than labelling an increasing number of young people as being 'disordered' or 'not normal', let's instead expect and accept this neurodiversity, anticipate these diverse needs and make it totally normal to be different. The benefits of this approach are enormous.

Victoria Honeybourne
November 2017

ACKNOWLEDGEMENTS

I would like to thank the many people who have been so willing to share their ideas, insights and expertise with me during the writing of this book – teachers, support staff, other professionals and young people themselves. In particular, I would like to thank my former colleagues on the Learning Support Advisory Team at Telford and Wrekin Council for their support and encouragement, and my colleagues on nasen's 11–25 Advisory Group for their ideas and enthusiasm.

CONTENTS

ABOUT THIS BOOK

There are many types of flowers. Daffodils, roses, lilies, daisies, tulips, bluebells, orchids – all different and all beautiful. We do not consider any one type of flower superior to any other. We do not try to make the rose more daffodil-like because we consider daffodils the best sort of flower. Flowers are not expected to be the same, but this natural variation is accepted and celebrated as part of biodiversity.

There are different types of everything – flowers, trees, birds, rocks – and, of course, people. Sometimes society can be less accepting of that fact. This book considers one specific type of human diversity, neurodiversity – the diversity of ways in which humans think, learn and relate to others. Some ways of being (such as those labelled with dyslexia or autism) are currently considered 'inferior' to other ways, rather than being expected and accepted as a natural aspect of human variation.

Going back to our flower analogy, different flowers need different conditions to thrive and flourish. Some need a sunny position, others do best in the shade. Some need regular watering, others survive with very little. Some flourish in clay soil, others in sandy, chalky or silty ground. Some grow very quickly, others take their time to flower. I once tried to grow edelweiss (a white Alpine mountain flower) in an English back garden. I was unsuccessful; the climatic and environmental conditions were not right. There was nothing wrong with the seeds, they simply did not have the environment they needed to thrive.

People are the same. Different people flourish in different environments. It makes sense; if we are all different, we will not all respond in the same way to the same inputs around us.

Our school systems, workplaces and society in general, have been designed for just one type of person – 'the neurotypical' – immediately placing any others at a disadvantage. When growing flowers, we have limited control over the weather and environment but, luckily, schools are different. They are man-made systems and as such we have total control over them. We can adapt the physical environment, we can change policies, we can adjust the way we communicate. We can recognise that neurodiversity exists and that our existing policies and practices have not been designed to meet the full range of this diversity.

In this book you will learn more about neurodiversity and how you can meet the needs of the neurodiverse student population in your schools and classrooms.

AIM OF THE BOOK

The aim of this book is to propose the neurodiversity paradigm as an effective way of approaching the issues of special educational needs and inclusion in schools in the twenty-first century.

IN THIS BOOK YOU WILL LEARN

- what is meant by the term 'neurodiversity'
- why the education system will benefit from adopting the neurodiversity paradigm
- the benefits of using the neurodiversity paradigm and how it can make a positive difference to teachers, students, families and communities
- how to adopt the neurodiversity paradigm in your educational setting
- easy-to-implement strategies which will support the neurodiverse student population to participate, learn and thrive.

WHO THIS BOOK IS FOR

Anybody working in primary and secondary schools:

- Head teachers

- Senior leadership teams

- SENCOs/ALNCOs (special/additional educational needs co-ordinators)

- Class teachers

- Teaching assistants

- Specialist/outreach teachers

- Student mentors/counsellors

- Trainee teachers

- SEN specialists

- Disability/inclusion advisors

USING THIS BOOK

To learn more about the concept of neurodiversity, begin with Chapters 1 and 2 ('Introducing Neurodiversity' and 'Understanding Neurodiversity'). To learn how to put the approach into practice, read Chapters 3 to 8. Chapter 8, 'Whole School Approaches', considers whole school policies and practices, as well as staff development. Chapter 4, 'Getting the Environment Right', considers how to make the physical environment within your setting more neurodiverse-friendly. Chapter 5, 'Teaching and Learning', explores inclusive teaching strategies and resources, as well as adult communication strategies, developing independence and meeting individual learning needs. Chapter 6, 'Student Wellbeing', considers how to promote happiness, resilience and positive attitudes in a neurodiverse student population and is followed by Chapter 7, 'Working with Home'.

Lists of commonly used abbreviations and signposting to further resources are included at the end of this book.

Useful forms in Chapters 6, 7 and 8 are available as downloads from www.jkp.com/voucher using the code MEERUGE.

1

INTRODUCING NEURODIVERSITY

In this chapter you will learn:

- what is meant by 'neurodiversity' and 'the neurodiversity paradigm'
- key terminology relating to neurodiversity
- how neurodiversity relates to existing models of disability
- why it is time to shift perspective when considering special educational needs and inclusion
- the benefits of using the neurodiversity paradigm in education.

INTRODUCTION

This book takes a new approach to the issue of special educational needs (SEN) and inclusion in schools: that of the neurodiversity paradigm. Let's start by considering why a new approach is needed.

There are more children and young people than ever before being diagnosed as having various neurodevelopmental conditions (such as dyslexia, attention deficit hyperactivity disorder (ADHD) or autism spectrum conditions) and many are consequently identified as having SEN. Most teachers now find themselves with a diverse population of students in their classrooms. In any one class you may have students with diagnoses of autism, ADHD, dyslexia, dyspraxia, obsessive compulsive disorder (OCD), pathological demand avoidance (PDA) and developmental language disorder, to name just a few! This can seem overwhelming to many teachers and school leaders. How is it possible to meet so many different needs in one classroom, particularly in times of limited staffing and resources? How can busy teachers, usually with no prior training in psychology or disability, be expected to learn about all of these conditions?

Many children and young people with identified neuro-developmental conditions are still experiencing difficulties in education – with parents feeling their child's needs are not being met, or students not fulfilling their potential. In our open and diverse twenty-first-century society we still marginalise and pathologise those who think differently, or who do not conform to narrow ideals of 'normal'. It is time for a new approach.

MODELS OF DISABILITY

Students with identified conditions and differences in the way that they learn are often deemed to have 'special educational needs', meaning that they need provision 'additional to or different from that made generally for other children or young people at the same school' (Department for Education 2015, p.16) in order to make progress and to access the curriculum. The term 'special educational needs' is often linked with a medical model of disability (Hodkinson 2016).

MEDICAL MODEL OF DISABILITY

In the medical model, special needs are understood to arise from psychological, neurological or physiological limitation within an individual. Through screening and assessment, children's deficits are labelled and described using clinical terminology (Skidmore 1996). Children are judged against 'developmental' and 'functional' norms (Hodkinson 2016) of other children their age.

The medical model of disability implies that there is something 'wrong' with individuals who are given a diagnosis depending on their symptoms. The medical model suggests that the individual can be fixed, treated, cured or ameliorated through medication, therapies or intervention. Criticisms of this model focus on the fact that it locates the problem within the individual and fails to take into account wider societal factors. The medical model also implies that there is one type of 'normal' and that those who deviate from this are 'abnormal' or need to be fixed to be more 'normal'.

Although the medical model is still widely used in education and health systems today, towards the end of the twentieth century the social model of disability began to gain wider recognition.

SOCIAL MODEL OF DISABILITY

Within this framework, society is considered to cause disability and special needs by placing barriers in the way of people with impairments (Goering 2010). It is not medical conditions that cause disability but the attitudes, values and beliefs operating within society. It is society that needs to be treated and cured, not individuals (Johnstone 2001).

The social model of disability proposes that individuals are only 'disabled' by the environments and attitudes around them. This social model has now become accepted and embedded in many elements of society. There are, however, also criticisms of this model. Opponents argue that the social model implies that physical differences and restrictions are entirely socially created. The social model has also been criticised for presenting disabled people as one homogeneous group, rather than as a complex group of individuals (Oliver 2013).

Some claim that neither the medical nor social models go far enough and that both obscure the real issues of oppression, discrimination and inequality (Oliver 1990). To overcome these issues, other theories of disability have also been proposed, such as the affirmative model and the rights-based model.

AFFIRMATIVE MODEL OF DISABILITY

The affirmative model promotes a non-tragic view of disability and impairment, promoting positive social identities for disabled people (Swain and French 2000). This model extends the social model by incorporating the lived experiences of disabled people (Johnstone 2001). It also opposes the assumption that disabled people want to be cured and challenges societal presumptions of what it means to be 'normal' (Swain and French 2004). The movement seeks to develop an image of disabled people that is 'strong, angry and proud' (Hodkinson 2016, p.34).

RIGHTS-BASED MODEL OF DISABILITY

The rights-based model of disability seeks to take on employers, policy-makers, educational and health care professionals to ensure that disabled people's rights are upheld. Disability politics seeks to liberate the 'silent' voices of disabled people and to confront the non-disabled 'oppressors who perpetuate the exclusion of disabled people' (Allen 2003, p.31). This model is about direct action and the use of the law to end discrimination against disabled people.

There are arguments for and against all these models of disability. Although social, affirmative and rights-based models are all gaining increasing recognition, it is still the medical model which dominates overwhelmingly in the current education system:

- Children and young people are identified as having special educational needs – the problem is diagnosed as being within the individual child (not as being a problem within the school or wider societal expectations).

- Children and young people are given labels and diagnoses depending on the symptoms or difficulties they are presenting with.

- A diagnosis of some sort is often required to access funding, resources or support in school, at home and in the community.

- The language used by educational and health care professionals is one of 'impairments', 'disorders' and 'pathology'.

- Children and young people are often placed in separate classes, interventions or groups depending on their 'label'.

- Children and young people are compared to 'normal' children of their age and to age-related expectations.

- The education system attempts to 'fix' children and young people who are not making the expected progress by giving them medication or an intervention to make them feel, think or act in a more 'appropriate' way.

- Targets set for many children and young people often focus on 'closing the gap' between them and their peers – suggesting that they should strive to be more 'normal' in all aspects of their development.

The early twenty-first century has brought huge changes in technological, cultural, political and societal spheres. We have more knowledge of neuroscience, biology and psychology than ever before. It is time for the education system to change the way it views disability and difference, and particularly to change attitudes towards neurodiversity.

WHAT IS NEURODIVERSITY?

NEURODIVERSITY

Neurodiversity (a term coined by Judy Singer in the 1990s and short for 'neurological diversity') simply means that there is a range, or diversity, of ways in which human brains function, a range of ways in which we think, learn and relate to others. Neurodiversity is a biological fact; we do not all think, learn and process information in the same way. Neurodiversity simply means that these neurological differences are a natural part of human variation.

The neurodiversity paradigm is a perspective on neurodiversity. It is based on the principle that neurodiversity is a natural form of human variation. The neurodiversity paradigm views the idea there is one 'right' type of brain or mind, or one 'right' way of neurocognitive functioning, as a culturally constructed fiction (Walker 2014).

Traditional view

Within the medical model, there is one 'right' way of neurocognitive functioning (neurotypical). Anybody who doesn't fit this profile is labelled as having something 'wrong' with them; they are viewed as 'abnormal', 'inferior' or 'disordered'.

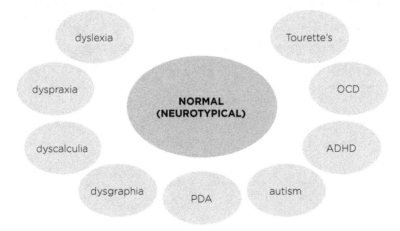

Neurodiversity paradigm

The concept of neurodiversity represents a paradigm shift for the fields of special educational needs and disability. Instead of pathologising individuals with perceived 'deficits' in the way that they think, learn and relate to others, the neurodiversity paradigm considers this diversity and variation of differences to be a normal, and totally expected, aspect of human variation. The neurodiversity paradigm sees that differences in neurocognitive functioning 'should be recognised as natural human variation instead of being pathologised' (Slorach 2016, p.212). This view sees traditional categories and labels of disability as social constructs and opposes the view that there is one 'normal' type of brain or one 'right' way of neurocognitive functioning. The term was originally used within the autistic community to reflect the idea that autism is not a disorder, merely a different way of being, and is now used in a wider sense to include all neurological differences – ways of being that we may label with terms such as autism, ADHD, dyslexia, dyscalculia, dyspraxia, Tourette syndrome (Tourette's) or other labels are all seen as being part of natural human neurodiversity.

In the neurodiversity paradigm no one way of neurocognitive functioning is considered to be superior to any other; all are equally valid. It is normal, and totally expected, that there will be this diversity and difference within the human race.

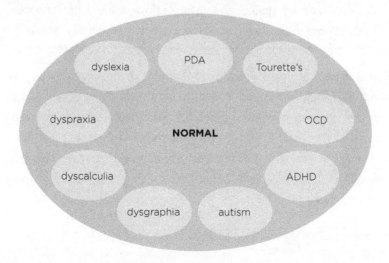

The concept of neurodiversity is refreshingly liberating: there is no normal; no one group is superior to any other; it is normal to be different.

TERMINOLOGY

Some key terms related to the concept of neurodiversity are:

- **Neurotypical (NT)**: Having a style of neurocognitive functioning which falls within the current dominant societal standards of 'normal'. Somebody without a 'label' or diagnosis of anything is classed as 'neurotypical'.

- **Neurodivergent**: Having a style of neurocognitive functioning which does not fall within the dominant societal standards of 'normal'. At the present time, anybody with a label or diagnosis (such as autism or dyslexia, for example) is considered to be neurodivergent.

- **Neurodiverse**: A group is neurodiverse if multiple ways of neurocognitive functioning are represented within the group.

- **Neurocognitive**: Relating to the mental processes which take place in the brain (e.g. the abilities to process, remember and retrieve information).

Throughout this book the terms 'neurotypical' and 'neurodivergent' are avoided as much as possible in order to move away from the idea that there are 'typical' and 'divergent' ways of being; this book firmly takes the approach that all ways of being are equally 'normal'!

Please note: The neurodiversity paradigm is not suggesting that conditions such as dyslexia, autism or dyspraxia do not exist, simply that they need to be viewed differently. The neurodiversity paradigm recognises that there is a huge variety of ways in which we think, learn and relate to others – and that this diversity needs to be recognised, anticipated and accepted, rather than being considered inferior or disordered.

BENEFITS OF THE NEURODIVERSITY PARADIGM

We have discussed what is meant by neurodiversity, so why is it time for this shift in the field of special educational needs and what are the benefits of moving towards the neurodiversity paradigm?

1 In the twenty-first century other types of diversity are accepted and celebrated; neurodiversity should be no different

In twenty-first-century Britain a wide range of diversities and differences are recognised, accepted and, indeed, celebrated. Cultural diversity, gender diversity, religious diversity and linguistic diversity are all part of everyday life. Attitudes have changed enormously over the past half century and we generally live in a much more tolerant and open society, in which citizens have the freedom and opportunity to be respected as individuals. Neurodiversity is simply another aspect of human diversity and should be recognised as such.

2 The increase in the number of children and young people diagnosed with various conditions and labels suggests that there is no 'normal' anyway

If we look at the statistics, we can see that a growing proportion of the population are receiving diagnoses and labels of various conditions and thus being labelled as neurodivergent.

- 10% of the population is dyslexic (BDA n.d.).

- 7% of children have a developmental language disorder (Communication Trust 2014).

- 5% of the population are thought to have dyscalculia (BDA 2015).

- 3% of the population are thought to be affected by developmental co-ordination disorder/dyspraxia (National Health Service 2016a).

- 2–5% of school-aged children may have ADHD (National Health Service 2016b).

- 1.1% of the population may have autism (National Autistic Society 2017).

The figures above do not take co-morbidity (co-occurrence) into account, but it is clear that it is no small minority of the student population who are neurodivergent. Some suggestions indicate that around 20 per cent of high school students in America are neurodivergent (Elder Robison 2015). There are also, perhaps, many more individuals who share similar characteristics but do not quite meet the criteria for a formal diagnosis. To say that this large proportion of the population are 'disordered', highlights a very narrow view of 'normality'.

3 The very act of labelling marginalises these groups and has a negative impact on individuals affected, as well as their families

The moment a group is labelled as being different, disordered or atypical, they are automatically marginalised. The act of diagnosing neurodevelopmental conditions places the blame firmly within the individual, suggesting that there is something 'wrong' with them. This can have a devastating effect on the individual in question, leading to low self-esteem and self-worth and to mental health conditions such as anxiety and depression.

For many individuals with neurocognitive functioning styles such as autism, ADHD and dyslexia, the issue is that these conditions are impossible to separate from the rest of the individual's personality. Our neurocognitive functioning style influences how we interpret the world, how we relate to others, how we learn and who we are. It pervades every aspect of our life. Being neurodivergent is something we are born with, not something that suddenly occurs and can be 'fixed' to revert us to 'normal'. This is why many neurodivergent individuals oppose the medical model of disability – to want to cure or fix us would be to want to change our make-up, our being, fundamentally who we are. Neurodevelopmental conditions are not a mental illness, they are a way of being.

4 Current terminology spreads stereotyping and prejudice

Labelling a group of individuals identifies them as being 'different'. The terminology around many types of special educational needs reinforces the medical model of disability – children and young people are told they have 'disorders'. Many terms – autism, ADHD, dyslexia, for example – also have negative connotations, often stereotyped and reinforced by the media. Within the general population, for example, many associate having ADHD with being naughty, or having dyslexia as being unintelligent.

Other stereotypes and prejudices regarding special needs and disabilities also prevail. The media often reinforces the fact that disabled people have 'something wrong with them', for example, by implying that they need to be 'pitied' and 'helped' (Swain and French 2000), that they 'bravely manage' despite impairments or that they are experiencing some sort of loss or tragedy and would prefer to be 'normal'.

Indeed, even the term 'special educational needs' has developed negative connotations and associations. Many argue that the term, which was originally coined in the late 1970s to move away from categorising children, does nothing more than introduce a new category (Terzi 2005). Others argue that the term 'special educational needs' lacks clarity, and is associated with difficulties in decision making (Frederickson and Cline 2009). The term can also be used negatively amongst young people themselves, with the term 'special' having derogatory undertones.

Further confusion occurs with the terms 'special needs' and 'special educational needs' – not all children with special needs will necessarily have special educational needs (Hodkinson 2016).

Educational professionals themselves can often be confused by the two, which can have serious consequences, such as lower expectations for children who have English as an Additional Language (a special need but not necessarily a special educational need) or difficulty planning support (Frederickson and Cline 2002).

The language we use has a huge influence on our thoughts, attitudes and opinion – it is, therefore, time to move away from a model of education which labels so negatively.

5 Traditional labels and categories of special educational needs are not necessary helpful; they tell us very little about individuals

A further argument for moving towards the neurodiversity paradigm is that current labels and categories of special educational needs in fact tell us very little about individuals within that category. 'Diagnostic categories are imperfect since they imply uniformity and clear-cut boundaries' (Grant 2017, p.172). Take the autism spectrum as an example. Individuals with a diagnosis of an autism spectrum condition (ASC; or 'disorder', ASD) can range from individuals who are articulate, intelligent, able to live independently and able to work, needing perhaps only minimal support to function in a world which has not been designed for them (often called Asperger syndrome or ASD Level 1), to individuals who are non-verbal, unable to communicate their needs, have additional learning difficulties and need significant, lifelong support (ASD Level 3). Even within these sub-categories of autism there can be huge differences. Much recent research, for example, is highlighting the differences between how males and females on the autism spectrum cope with their differences. So the term 'autism' may not actually be helpful at all and can tell educational professionals very little about the student in front of them. The same is relevant for dyslexia, dyspraxia or ADHD for example – each individual will experience the condition differently and will have their own combination of strengths, difficulties, coping strategies and experiences. Far better is to have an approach which focuses on individuality rather than a group identity, an approach which meets the needs of individuals, not the label.

6 Educators and other support staff can feel overwhelmed by the current system

'I have one with ADHD, one with autism, one with dyslexia, one with ODD and a few with language needs. How can I meet all their needs in one classroom? I'll have to do so many different things for them.' (Year 4 class teacher)

'A child in my class has ADHD and autism. The ADHD literature tells me to keep activities short and varied, but the autism advice says to focus on just one thing and have slow, clear transitions between activities. What do I follow?' (Year 7 English teacher)

'I can't overload my staff with information. We've had training on ADHD this year. That's enough for now.' (Secondary school SENCO)

'We can't do dyslexia-friendly environments this year as we are doing autism-friendly environments.' (Primary school SENCO)

'Our teachers have enough to do without having to become experts in dyslexia, autism, ADHD, OCD, PDA and all the other conditions that children are coming to us with. There isn't the time or money to train them all up in everything.' (Secondary school deputy head)

Attitudes like these indicate that the average educational professional can feel overwhelmed by the current special educational needs system. The myth perpetuates that a myriad of teaching approaches is necessary according to different identified conditions and diagnoses within a class (Herbert 2011). Many teachers mistakenly believe that children with different labels all need wildly different teaching styles.

It is, therefore, time to move away from a system which categorises and classifies, towards one which sees neurodiversity as a natural aspect of human variation to be anticipated and expected.

7 Trying 'to fit square pegs into round holes' is an outdated concept and fails to take into account normal diversity

In the current education system, and indeed in society as a whole, there is often an increasing emphasis on normality. Young people are expected to learn in exactly the same way at the same rate. This focus can be extremely damaging for the growing number of young people who are told they are 'not meeting expected standards' or not making sufficient progress. This way of viewing young people fails to take into account the fact that as humans we are all different and learn in different ways – indeed, this diversity is what makes us human. It is what makes life so wonderfully interesting and varied.

To the twenty-first-century mind, it seems unacceptable that once, not so long ago, all children were forced to write with their right hand – left-handedness was considered to be 'wrong'! Yet there are similar attitudes in some parts of the education system today!

As adults we accept that we all learn in different ways. Think about learning to drive, for example. How long did it take you to learn? Six weeks, six months, six years, somewhere in between? Did you pass your test first time? Second time? Third time? What about your theory test? And did you learn from books, videos, online tests? How much practice did you need between lessons? What did you find hardest – parking, the theory, motorway driving? There would be as many answers to those questions as there are individuals, but the point is that the majority – however they learned and however long they needed – go on to be safe, competent drivers. Those that pass first time after just six weeks of lessons do not necessarily become the safest drivers. As adults we accept this variation – similarly we need to expect that children and young people will learn at different rates and in different ways.

8 Current systems fail to take into consideration that environments, policies and practices have only been designed for one type of brain, the 'neurotypical' way of thinking and learning

As already discussed, up until now a medical model of disability has prevailed in most education, health and care systems. This medical model does not take into consideration that the environment, policies and practices which surround us have generally only been designed for one way of thinking – for the neurotypical brain. This means that anybody considered 'neurodivergent' is automatically placed at a disadvantage from the beginning, no matter how hard they try.

By embracing the concept of neurodiversity, educational settings recognise that environments, policies and practices need to be designed to reflect the neurodiverse population that we are, rather than reinforce just one way of being as the 'right' way to be.

Many difficulties and problems that neurodivergent individuals experience often only come about because of the expectation to be 'neurotypical'. Remove these expectations and many problems automatically disappear.

9 Normal is a social construct and reflects only what is considered 'typical' at any particular time

A little over 50 years ago homosexuality was considered a mental illness and a criminal act in the UK. Sexual diversity is now widely recognised and accepted, with same-sex couples sharing the same rights as heterosexual couples. This illustrates how views of 'normal' change over time.

'Normal' is a social construct and reflects only current views and beliefs about what constitutes 'typical' or 'acceptable' in any particular place or time. What is normal in one culture may be considered abnormal in another. What is considered normal for one generation may be considered abnormal for another. It is, therefore, important not to place too much of an emphasis on being 'normal'. Indeed, there are arguments that even the International Classification of

Diseases and Related Health Problems, Version 10 (ICD-10) – used by many practitioners to diagnose – reflects a 'narrow, Eurocentric view of society that is firmly predicated upon the values of healthy, male, middle-class professionals' (Oliver and Barnes 1998, cited in Hodkinson 2016, p.50).

10 We are experiencing a collective shift in consciousness

Embracing the neurodiversity paradigm reflects the collective shift in consciousness we are experiencing. In recent years there has been a gradual shift away from the consumerism and commercialisation of the late twentieth century, with more and more people seeking deeper meaning and purpose, shedding the layers of social conditioning they realise have been causing unhappiness. We are experiencing a huge shift towards mindfulness, the 'slow' living movement, yoga, rewilding and simpler lifestyles. Pick up most magazines and newspapers and you are likely to find articles on decluttering, simplifying life, being mindful and living in the moment. This shift will see more people realise that the 'shoulds' they believe, the judgements they make and the beliefs they subscribe to are socially constructed and inflict unnecessary suffering. This collective move towards a simpler, more natural way of living means that as a society and culture we are more receptive to challenging previously held opinions – and to realising that there are many ways to be human, and that all are equally valid.

TIME TO EMBRACE NEURODIVERSITY

It can be challenging for individuals, settings, systems and societies to shift perspective and to start looking at things differently, but the benefits of using the neurodiversity paradigm are innumerable.

To summarise, this paradigm proposes that neurodiversity is a normal and natural aspect of human variation. It should be anticipated and expected that there is a diversity of ways in which humans think, learn and relate to others. The neurodiversity paradigm does not consider that there is one 'normal' way of being, and that everything else is deviant from this, but rather that all styles of neurocognitive functioning are equally valid. Neurodiversity should be recognised, accepted and valued. It is normal to be different; it is not normal for everybody to be the same.

Using the neurodiversity paradigm offers a refreshing perspective and brings many benefits:

- Individuals labelled as being 'disordered', 'abnormal' or 'inferior' benefit. Their individuality and differences are expected and anticipated as part of normal human variation. The neurodiversity paradigm removes stigma, stereotyping and prejudice. Individuals feel accepted, valued and just as important as anybody else, rather than growing up believing it is not ok to be who they are.

- All children and young people benefit from growing up and being educated in a society which recognises and accepts difference of all kinds, rather than labelling and marginalising certain groups. More accepting and open-minded attitudes in one sphere of life spill into other areas too.

- Families of neurodivergent individuals also benefit. Having a child with special educational needs can be difficult; many families find themselves having to dedicate a lot of time to fighting for a diagnosis, for support, for needs to be met within the school system. Many also have to contend with negative attitudes from others. Having a child or young person who believes there is something 'wrong' with them, who has low self-esteem, who is deemed 'different', can have an impact on family dynamics. Far better if the educational system, families and society as a whole expect and anticipate neurodiversity. If schools are already geared up to meeting the needs of a neurodiverse student population, much time, energy and frustration are saved.

- Educational professionals also benefit from shifting their perspective. Rather than feeling overwhelmed by the concept of special educational needs and feeling that children with SEN mean extra work, a school or classroom which is neurodiverse-friendly meets many needs in general day-to-day good practice. A neurodiverse student population is inevitable – this needs to be planned for, not reacted to.

- Generally, society and culture as a whole benefit from shifting to the neurodiversity paradigm. Recognising neurodiversity reduces stigma, discrimination and prejudice for adults as well as children. It improves wellbeing and acceptance for everybody. Simply removing the expectation to be 'neurotypical' eliminates and reduces many of the difficulties, problems and suffering which exist.

This chapter has outlined what is meant by neurodiversity and why it is beneficial for the educational system to shift towards using the neurodiversity paradigm. The next chapter explores neurodiversity in more detail; the chapters which follow outline how to put the approach into practice in educational settings.

KEY POINTS

- Neurodiversity simply means that there is a range, or diversity, of ways in which human beings think, learn and relate to others. It is normal to be different!

- The neurodiversity paradigm proposes that all of these ways of neurocognitive functioning are equally valid; no one way is superior to any other. This is in contrast to the medical model of disability, which proposes that there is 'normal' and that anybody who deviates from this is 'abnormal' and labelled with a disorder such as autism, dyslexia, dyspraxia or ADHD.

- There are many benefits of using the neurodiversity paradigm: for children and young people, for their families, for schools and for society as a whole.

- A shift to the neurodiversity paradigm is needed for the rest of the twenty-first century; current conceptualisations of special educational needs are unsustainable and unhelpful. Many educational professionals currently feel overwhelmed and many students are unable to participate, achieve or experience a state of wellbeing and acceptance.

2

UNDERSTANDING NEURODIVERSITY

In this chapter you will learn:

- how exactly humans are 'neurodiverse'; how some individuals think, learn and relate differently to others

- about traditional diagnostic categories and how these relate to the concept of neurodiversity

- about other types of diversity relating to children and young people in educational settings

- the importance of adopting the neurodiversity paradigm as an approach.

In the previous chapter we learned what is meant by the term neurodiversity. We are now going to consider this diversity in more detail. Neurodiversity means that humans will think, learn, process information and relate to others in a diversity of ways – but what does this diversity look like?

This book is not about labels and diagnoses; indeed, we are trying to move away from an approach which labels individuals with 'disorders' and 'abnormalities' and towards an inclusive approach which recognises that there is no normal. However, in this part of the book it is necessary to look first at current categories and labels that neurodivergent individuals are given, in order to understand the range of neurodiversity. We will consider: dyslexia, dysgraphia, dyspraxia, dyscalculia, autism spectrum conditions, PDA, ADHD and developmental language disorder.

DYSLEXIA

Definition

'Dyslexia is a learning difficulty that primarily affects the skills involved in accurate and fluent word reading and spelling. Characteristic features of dyslexia are difficulties in phonological awareness, verbal memory and verbal processing speed. Dyslexia occurs across the range of intellectual abilities. It is best thought of as a continuum, not a distinct category, and there are no clear cut-off points' (Rose Report 2009, p.9). It is thought to affect up to 10 per cent of the population, with severity varying from individual to individual (BDA n.d.).

Characteristics

Students with dyslexia may:

- have slow reading speed
- read inaccurately (particularly when under pressure)
- misread words for similar-looking words (e.g. 'staring' for 'starting')
- not always understand or be able to keep track of what they are reading (as they are concentrating so hard on deciphering the words)
- experience discomfort when reading
- feel overwhelmed by large amounts of text
- avoid reading aloud
- become frustrated when reading
- experience difficulty acquiring phonics
- have inconsistent spelling
- confuse sounds and letters
- reverse letters and numerals
- copy words and spellings inaccurately from other sources
- find it difficult to keep up with note-taking and dictation
- avoid writing words that are difficult to spell

- have difficulty in organising their thoughts clearly and logically

- experience difficulty with letter formation and handwriting

- have poor short-term memory (e.g. remembering instructions and information, retaining numbers for calculations, remembering what to write down)

- take longer to process information (both spoken and written) before responding

- appear to be disorganised

- have a poor sense of direction

- confuse right and left

- misread timetables and instructions

- have difficulty telling the time

- have difficulty with remembering sequences (e.g. the months of the year, the days of the week)

- forget equipment and belongings

- have low self-esteem

- find school exhausting as they have to work harder than other students to keep up

- have slow writing speed.

Remember that not all students will experience all of these difficulties. As with any condition, dyslexia is considered to be a continuum with individuals affected to different degrees.

Dyslexia is considered to be a neurodevelopmental condition which specifically affects the acquisition of reading and writing. There are many other children and young people who also experience reading difficulties for other reasons (such as missed schooling, inappropriate teaching methods or weak early language skills). They might experience some of the same difficulties in the classroom and many strategies can benefit both groups.

Visual stress (also sometimes called Irlen syndrome or Meares-Irlen syndrome) can often be confused with dyslexia. Individuals who have visual stress experience 'visual distortions when looking at a page of text' (Grant 2017, p.115). Text may appear to be moving or jumping, words may merge into each other and white paper may seem to 'glare', making reading difficult. There may be particular difficulties with small fonts or with reading black text on white paper. Individuals with visual stress may also experience migraines or find it difficult to read in brightly lit environments. Although visual stress can occur with dyslexia, it also affects many individuals without dyslexia and is considered a visual difficulty; assessment should come from a qualified optometrist. Visual stress can often be reduced by using a coloured overlay, tinted lenses or printing onto pastel-coloured paper. Individuals may need a specialist assessment to discover which colour they benefit from.

DYSGRAPHIA
Definition

'Dysgraphia affects handwriting and converting thoughts to written words. People with dysgraphia are within the normal intelligence range but they struggle to put their ideas down clearly and coherently on paper. Their writing may be illegible or untidy despite considerable effort and there is a disparity between ideas and understanding expressed verbally and those presented in writing' (Hudson 2016, p.75).

Dysgraphia can be a contentious term and is not as widely recognised as conditions such as dyslexia and dyspraxia. Confusion can occur as there can be many reasons for handwriting problems: motor difficulties, spatial and visual processing difficulties or difficulties visualising the appearance of letters.

It is important to remember that dysgraphia is more than simply untidy handwriting. Dysgraphia affects a person's ability to write quickly, fluently and effortlessly, meaning they might be unable to demonstrate what they know or to show their potential.

Characteristics

Students with dysgraphia may:

- have untidy handwriting, despite trying hard

- have a slow writing speed

- tire quickly when writing

- find it difficult to write on the lines or to keep a margin

- use inconsistent spacing between words and letters

- have difficulty with letter formation, reverse some letters or mix upper and lower case letters

- repeat or omit words and letters

- have weak spelling and punctuation

- not be able to join letters

- have inconsistent handwriting

- produce work which is poorly presented, despite their best efforts

- have difficulty reading maps or following directions

- find it difficult to draw diagrams, graphs, shapes and lay out maths problems

- experience physical discomfort when handwriting

- have an unusual pencil grip or body position for handwriting

- experience other difficulties with fine motor skills

- need to concentrate when writing, meaning they are unable to process other information at the same time

- find it hard to structure sentences and to organise their thoughts logically on paper

- be able to express themselves well verbally but be unable to get their thoughts down on paper

- may underperform on written tests, examinations and homework tasks
- become frustrated with writing tasks
- avoid written tasks where possible
- have low self-esteem.

DYSCALCULIA
Definition

Dyscalculia is a specific learning difficulty which affects counting, arithmetic and learning mathematical skills. As a specific learning difficulty, dyscalculia is different from mathematical difficulties which arise from educational experiences or a general learning disability.

Characteristics

Students with dyscalculia may:

- not have an intuitive knowledge of the number system
- have difficulty counting
- need to count items in a group individually every time they see them (e.g. dice patterns)
- often use their fingers to count
- have difficulty with rounding numbers up or down and with estimation
- find it difficult to understand which number is larger or smaller than another
- confuse similar-looking numbers (6 and 9) or similar-sounding numbers (13 and 30) or reverse numbers (451 for 415)
- take considerably longer than their peers to learn number facts, such as times tables

- not see connections between number relationships (e.g. not see the relationships between addition and subtraction or the patterns of place value)

- experience difficulty learning and remembering mathematical procedures

- follow mathematical procedures without understanding the concepts behind them

- find it difficult to understand percentages, fractions and decimals

- misread mathematical symbols

- not be able to answer mental maths problems

- have difficulty remembering number sequences

- experience difficulty with telling the time or using money

- find shape, direction and orientation difficult

- feel frustrated, anxious and lack confidence when doing maths and in subjects which require using numbers (e.g. science, geography, cooking and technology)

- have low self-esteem.

Again, there can also be other students who experience difficulties with maths for many reasons (such as inappropriate teaching methods, missed schooling or language difficulties). They may demonstrate similar challenges and difficulties and, again, many strategies can be beneficial for both groups.

DYSPRAXIA (ALSO CALLED DEVELOPMENTAL CO-ORDINATION DISORDER)
Definition

'Dyspraxia, otherwise known as Developmental Coordination Disorder (DCD) is a common disorder affecting fine and/or gross motor skills coordination, in both children and adults. The Dyspraxia

Foundation adds to this, recognising the many non-motor difficulties that may also be experienced by people with the condition and which can have a significant impact on daily life activities. These include memory, perception and processing as well as additional problems with planning, organising and carrying out movements in the right order in everyday situations. Dyspraxia can also affect articulation and speech' (Dyspraxia Foundation 2015).

Characteristics

Students with dyspraxia may:

- have poor co-ordination
- appear clumsy
- have poor spatial awareness
- find it challenging to use equipment such as scissors, a ruler or other tools
- easily bump into things or trip over
- need extra time to get dressed, undressed and complete other tasks which use motor skills
- find it difficult to catch, throw or kick a ball
- have poor balance
- have untidy handwriting
- experience discomfort when handwriting and when using instruments such as a ruler
- have poor posture
- have an unusual gait when walking, running, skipping or jumping
- not be aware of personal space – stand too close or too far away from others
- find it difficult to remember instructions
- have poor organisational skills
- experience difficulty with time management
- have a poor sense of direction

- forget equipment
- produce written work which is disorganised or unstructured
- need additional time to process information
- have poor short-term visual and verbal memory (e.g. for instructions, copying from the board or dictation)
- have difficulty sequencing information
- be under- or over-sensitive to sensory inputs such as light, sound, taste, smell or touch
- be less emotionally mature than their peer group
- have difficulty reading body language
- find it difficult to pick up on implied or inferred information
- take language literally
- experience difficulties forming and maintaining friendships
- not 'fit in with the crowd'
- behave immaturely for their chronological age
- try to avoid sports or other practical subjects
- appear socially awkward
- feel embarrassed by the physical challenges
- have low self-esteem.

AUTISM SPECTRUM CONDITIONS (INCLUDING ASPERGER SYNDROME)
Definition

'Autism is a lifelong developmental disability that affects how people perceive the world and interact with others. Autistic people see, hear and feel the world differently to other people. Often people feel being autistic is a fundamental aspect of their identity. Some autistic people say the world feels overwhelming and this can cause them considerable anxiety. In particular, understanding and relating to other people, and taking part in everyday family, school, work and social life, can be harder' (National Autistic Society 2016).

Autism is a spectrum condition and, although all autistic people share similar difficulties, they will all be affected in different ways. The characteristics of autism differ from person to person but to receive a diagnosis, individuals will have difficulties in two main areas: persistent difficulties with social interaction and communication and restricted and repetitive patterns of behaviours, activities and interests. These difficulties will have been present since early childhood and will 'limit and impair everyday functioning' (National Autistic Society 2016).

Asperger syndrome is a type of autism. People with Asperger syndrome experience the same difficulties as others on the autism spectrum, however they do not have the learning difficulties that others on the autism spectrum may have. They can be of average or above-average intelligence and may have fewer problems with speech, although they will still experience difficulties with processing and understanding language. The term 'Asperger syndrome' is currently being replaced with the term 'Autism spectrum disorder Level 1'.

Characteristics

Students on the autism spectrum may:

- have difficulty interpreting verbal and non-verbal language

- take things literally and find it difficult to understand sarcasm and jokes

- find it difficult to understand tone of voice or facial expression

- struggle with vagueness or abstract concepts

- have difficulty understanding the dynamics of group conversation (such as when it is their turn to talk, how to interrupt appropriately or how to change topic)

- talk at length about their own interests

- find small talk difficult

- repeat what other people have said (echolalia)

- appear pedantic in their speech

- lack facial expression and have limited variety in their tone of voice

- find eye contact uncomfortable

- need additional processing time to make sense of what is being said

- have difficulty in understanding other people's perspectives, thoughts and feelings (sometimes called difficulties with 'theory of mind')

- have difficulty in recognising, understanding and expressing their own emotions

- prefer to work alone

- find working with others difficult

- appear to be insensitive

- need and prefer considerable alone time

- not connect with others on a social level

- not seek comfort from others in expected ways

- appear to act in a socially inappropriate way

- appear socially awkward

- find it difficult to make and maintain friendships

- prefer routines, timetables and structure

- dislike change and unpredictability

- appear to have inflexible thought patterns and attitudes

- be rule-orientated

- be very honest

- unintentionally cause offence

- have highly focused, intense interests (special interests)

- be over- or under-sensitive to sensory stimulus such as noise, light, taste, smell and touch

- find sensory input painful

- be unable to block out background noise

- have some repetitive behaviour patterns

- become frustrated with unfairness

- experience constant anxiety

- feel 'different' from others

- feel misunderstood and isolated

- have low self-esteem.

PATHOLOGICAL DEMAND AVOIDANCE (PDA)
Definition

Pathological demand avoidance (PDA) is a profile which is increasingly being considered to be part of the autism spectrum. Individuals with PDA can share some of the same characteristics as those on the autism spectrum, however, they are driven to avoid everyday demands and expectations to an extreme extent due to an anxiety-based need to be in control (National Autistic Society 2016). Individuals with PDA generally have better social interaction and communication than others on the autism spectrum.

Characteristics

Students with PDA may:

- resist and avoid demands of everyday life

- use social strategies, such as giving excuses or distraction, as a means of avoiding tasks

- appear sociable but lack understanding

- appear to use appropriate social communication skills

- have difficulty processing and understanding information

- experience excessive mood swings

- experience sudden anger outbursts

- act impulsively

- appear comfortable in role play and pretence

- display obsessive behaviour focused on other people

- appear controlling or dominating

- appear to want everything on their own terms

- perceive suggestions as demands

- appear social at first

- be able to adapt different strategies to different people

- have difficulty taking responsibility for their actions

- display confusing behaviours or contradictory moods

- lack a sense of embarrassment or pride

- become overfamiliar and bossy

- display other behaviours characteristic of the autism spectrum (see above).

Although PDA is increasingly being seen as part of the autism spectrum, many parents and professionals find that autism-friendly strategies are less effective with these children as those with a PDA profile need a less directive and more flexible approach than others on the autism spectrum. PDA is not yet as widely understood as other autism spectrum conditions and it is important to remember that students with PDA are not making a deliberate choice not to comply and cannot overcome their need to be in control – their behaviours are driven by extreme anxiety.

ATTENTION DEFICIT HYPERACTIVITY DISORDER (ADHD)
Definition

ADHD can be characterised by inattention, hyperactivity and impulsiveness, with individuals affected in different ways. In order for a diagnosis to be given, individuals will usually demonstrate difficulties in at least two different settings (e.g. school and home), symptoms will have been present before the age of 12 and difficulties will have a significant negative impact on everyday life.

There are different types of ADHD – predominantly inattentive ADHD, predominantly hyperactive impulsive ADHD and combined ADHD. As with all neurodevelopmental conditions, individuals are affected to different degrees. Some individuals with ADHD manage their condition with medication.

Characteristics

Students with ADHD may:

- fidget, appear restless, move a lot
- need to get up and move around
- find it difficult to relax and stay still
- be easily distracted
- have a short attention span
- daydream
- find it difficult to concentrate and to focus
- not be able to listen to, remember or follow instructions
- rush tasks or begin them before listening to all of the instructions
- be slow completing tasks
- have poor organisational skills
- forget and lose equipment
- have difficulty with short-term memory
- not complete tasks
- talk excessively
- appear 'silly' or immature in their behaviour and attitude
- demonstrate impulsive behaviour
- not appear to recognise danger
- shout out
- be impatient
- become angry or aggressive
- interrupt
- have difficulty with planning and time management

- find it difficult to wait

- not learn from experience

- not consider the consequences of their behaviour

- not make rational decisions

- have difficulty making and maintaining friendships

- inadvertently irritate and annoy their peers

- appear emotionally and socially immature compared to their peers

- have low self-esteem as they find it difficult to complete tasks and experience success.

Children do not 'grow out' of ADHD, or any other neurodivergent way of being, although many individuals learn effective coping strategies and learn how to make the most of their individuality and strengths. Some older adolescents and adults with ADHD may display some of the following:

- procrastination

- mood instability

- low self-esteem

- underachievement

- intolerance of boredom

- trouble completing tasks

- sense of insecurity

- inaccurate self-observation and assessment of others.

(Adapted from O'Regan 2007, p.23)

DEVELOPMENTAL LANGUAGE DISORDER (DLD)
Definition

Developmental language disorder is the term given to children who experience difficulty acquiring language in the absence of any other difficulties which could explain this. DLD is the term given when there are no other known causes for language difficulties. Children and young people with conditions such as autism, ADHD, dyspraxia, dyslexia, hearing impairment and others can also experience difficulties with using and understanding language related to their primary need.

Children with DLD may experience difficulty with different aspects of language: understanding (receptive) language, using (expressive) language, grammar, vocabulary, or knowing when and how to use language in social situations (pragmatics).

Until recently, DLD was known as specific language impairment (SLI). The term DLD is now used to remove some of the assumptions and confusions that existed over the diagnosis of SLI (Afasic 2016).

Children with DLD can struggle at school, as language is the predominant means of teaching and learning. They might be intelligent in other ways but have difficulty in understanding and/or using language.

Characteristics

Students with DLD may:

- appear to be listening but do not seem to understand
- not follow instructions accurately
- seem to 'get the wrong end of the stick'
- have difficulty using and understanding vocabulary
- talk in short sentences
- talk in long sentences which are difficult to understand
- appear to have good ideas but be unable to express themselves coherently
- go off on a tangent when talking
- stick to talking about topics they feel comfortable with
- use set phrases they have learned or copied from others without really understanding what they mean
- answer off-topic
- become frustrated with not being able to express their thoughts and feelings

- have difficulty remembering the words they wanted to say

- struggle with inference or implied information

- be unable to give a clear and coherent account of what has happened

- have difficulty joining in group conversation

- have difficulty keeping up in class discussion or following what is going on

- not always be able to demonstrate their potential in written tests, exams and homework

- have related literacy difficulties with understanding and producing written texts

- find it hard to make and maintain friendships

- misunderstand other people's intentions and meanings

- have low self-esteem.

There can be some confusion with the terms 'speech' and 'language'. Speech is the physical process of making and articulating sounds. Children with speech difficulties, can be easier to spot than those with language difficulties, which can be more 'invisible' in the classroom. Children with speech difficulties may include those with dysfluency (a stammer or stutter), speech sound difficulties or voice disorders.

There are also many other children who experience speech, language and communication needs (SLCN) due to social deprivation or a language-poor background. These children have poor or immature language but have the potential to catch up with their peers. It is thought that approximately 50 per cent of children in some areas are starting school with language skills below those expected for their age (Law, McBean and Rush 2011).

MORE INCLUSIVE APPROACHES

In this chapter we have outlined some of the most common 'types' of neurodiversity: dyslexia, dysgraphia, dyscalculia, dyspraxia, autism spectrum conditions, PDA, ADHD and developmental language disorder. Unlike many books, however, this one does not go on to have different sections such as 'strategies for dyslexic students' or 'strategies for autistic students'. The emphasis instead is on moving away from categories which see some ways of being as 'disordered' and towards an approach which anticipates and expects a neurodiverse student population. There are other reasons why it can be unhelpful to focus on discrete categories:

- Many students have multiple diagnoses – such as ADHD and autism, or dyslexia and dyspraxia.

- No two students with the same diagnosis will have the same needs. Each student will have a different combination of difficulties and differences from the lists above. It is impossible to take a list of 'strategies for working with students with ADHD', for example, and assume that every strategy will be of use to every student.

- There is no clear cut-off point to each category, and students are affected to different degrees. Some students may have characteristics of a given condition but fail to meet all of the criteria for a formal diagnosis. This means that they may not always get the support they need as some institutions or professionals may recognise only formal diagnoses. A further issue is that support needs to be available from the outset – not only after lengthy assessment and diagnostic processes have taken place – by which time the student is already likely to have experienced difficulties and low self-esteem. In addition, there can be disparity between different geographical areas in terms of diagnostic services.

- There is also some evidence that girls may be less likely to receive various diagnoses due to how they cope with their differences and difficulties. Girls on the autism spectrum, for example, may be missed as they mask their difficulties through copying others (Honeybourne 2016) and use intellectual abilities rather than intuition (Attwood 2007).

Evidence also suggests that ADHD may not be recognised in as many girls as boys (Dray, Campbell and Gilmore 2006; Myttas 2009). The same phenomenon has been identified with both dyslexia (Siegel and Smythe 2005) and dyspraxia (Missiuna *et al.* 2006). Various factors could contribute to this lack of recognition: professional/teacher/parent bias, stereotypes, different gender expectations and how girls cope with difficulties compared to boys.

- As previously discussed, categories and labels can lead to stereotyping and changing expectations.

- Looking down a class list of 'labels and diagnoses' can feel overwhelming; many staff do not know where to start, or feel that they have to become an expert in each one.

You will see by now that a very individual approach is needed; we cannot simply look at a student's diagnosis and assume that we know all about the student and how best to support them. From reading the lists above, however, you will also see that there is a commonality for many students who fit these categories. For example, many individuals across these diagnoses experience some of the following:

- Difficulties with working memory ('the capacity to remember verbal information for a short period of time'; Grant 2017, p.10) can be common and can also vary with stress and anxiety levels. Difficulties with working memory can affect many areas of school life including participation and understanding in class, reading skills, written work, maths and organisation.

- Differences in processing speed and ability. Processing speed (the time it takes to process visual or verbal information) can also affect many academic areas, such as reading, writing, class discussion and particularly working under time constraints such as in tests and examinations.

- Differences with 'executive functioning' skills. Executive functioning includes skills such as planning, organising, structuring, prioritising, focusing attention, memory, managing time and other self-regulation skills.

- Differences in communication style. Individuals may have difficulties with communication – some may have difficulty understanding, others may not be able to express themselves well, while others may have difficulty with various aspects of social communication (such as conversational skills and non-verbal communication). Differences communicating can affect academic work, relationships with staff and relationships with peers. There may be difficulty in making and maintaining friendships.

- Many individuals with various diagnoses may also experience low self-esteem due to their difficulties, and as a result may also experience problems such as feeling isolated, left-out, frustrated, excluded, 'different', depressed or anxious.

This book focuses on commonality and individuality. First, it is important to recognise and accept that our student population is neurodiverse. We need to see this neurodiversity as an expected part of human variation, not as an inferiority. There are many things we can do to make our education system more accepting of our neurodiverse student body, rather than being biased towards only those who would be classed as 'neurotypical'. Many of the strategies and approaches outlined later in this book work on making school systems, policies and practices more inclusive – creating a communication-friendly environment in your setting, for example, will support students with a wide range of differences. You will discover that staff do not have to be an expert in each different named condition but that there are elements of good practice which can help many students (common approaches to support all).

The book also encourages schools to accept individuality and difference; not to expect every student to function, work and live in the same way (embracing and accepting individuality). The key message is that we need to anticipate and prepare for a more neurodiverse student population and realise that this diversity really will come in a multitude of individual forms! The remaining chapters in this book explain what this approach looks like in practice.

OTHER TYPES OF DIVERSITY

This book focuses on neurodiversity; the diversity of ways in which we think, learn, process information and relate to others. However, there are also many other types of diversity, disability and learning needs relevant to educational settings.

- **Linguistic diversity.** Students may have English as an Additional Language (EAL), meaning that English is not their first language. Some students may have learned English from a young age, others may arrive in the country with no previous experience of the language. Some students speak a language other than English at home and encounter English only when in school. There are also many native English-speaking children (up to and over 50% in some areas) who enter school with delayed language and communication skills (Law *et al.* 2011). All of these groups can experience language and communication difficulties in the school environment.

- **Cultural diversity.** Students come from a wide range of social, cultural and religious backgrounds, observing different customs, rituals, beliefs and values.

- **Gender and sexuality diversity.** Students will have different sexual orientations – heterosexual, homosexual, bisexual or asexual, for example. Gender identity is a person's internal understanding of their gender. This may correspond with the person's assigned sex, or it may not. A female, for example, may identify with being a male, or vice versa – this is often called transgender. Some may identify with being neither male nor female.

- **Physical and sensory needs.** Physical disabilities can affect mobility, movement, strength or speech. Sensory difficulties include visual or hearing impairment.

- **Medical needs.** Short-term or long-term medical conditions can include illnesses, allergies, epilepsy or injuries.

- **Global learning difficulties.** 'Global' or 'general' learning difficulties are very wide terms which refer to children and young people who have difficulties or delays in all aspects of their learning and development (academic learning, social and emotional development, communication skills). You may also hear terms such as 'severe learning difficulties', 'moderate learning difficulties' or 'mild learning difficulties', which relate to the severity of these difficulties.

- **Social, emotional and mental health needs (SEMH).** This is an overarching term for children and young people who have difficulties with emotional regulation and/or social interaction and/or who are experiencing mental health difficulties. These difficulties can occur for many different reasons, to different levels of severity, and can be short or long term. Examples of emotional and mental health difficulties can include attachment disorders, eating disorders, phobias, anxiety and depression.

These differences, diversities and disabilities all occur in the wider student population. 'Neurodivergent' students may also experience these additional differences, just as any other student. This book focuses on neurodiversity but many of the strategies and approaches outlined will also help students who identify with some of the above groups. Making a school more accepting of neurodiversity will support acceptance of all types of difference and disability and does not disadvantage any group of students.

REMEMBER – IT'S NOT JUST THE SENCO'S ISSUE!

Students with special/additional educational needs have often been seen to be the responsibility of the school's special educational needs co-ordinator (SENCO) or learning support department. However, the SEN Code of Practice (Department for Education 2015) makes it clear that all teachers are teachers of SEN and that class teachers are ultimately responsible for the progress of students in their class – including those who have SEN or who may be supported by a teaching assistant. Neurodiversity is inevitable in every classroom and affects the student population in every aspect of school life; every member of staff needs to be aware of this to ensure the most effective outcomes for students.

Having discussed what is meant by neurodiversity and how students can be 'neurodiverse', the remaining chapters of this book now consider practical strategies for the school and classroom.

KEY POINTS

- Neurodiversity encompasses many different ways of being. Traditional categories such as dyslexia, dyspraxia, dyscalculia, autism, ADHD and DLD can all be considered ways that the population can be neurodiverse.

- Traditional categories are not necessarily helpful – individuals all have different combinations of strengths and difficulties. Individuals are affected to different levels of severity.

- Students who can be classed as 'neurodivergent' often share some similar difficulties – for example, with low self-esteem, maintaining friendships, executive functioning skills, working memory, organisation or communication.

- The student population is diverse in many other ways too. Neurodiversity needs to be recognised and accepted in the same way as other types of diversity. Getting it right for a neurodiverse student population will help everybody and disadvantage nobody.

3

COMMUNICATION

In this chapter you will learn:

- the importance of communication in education and where breakdowns can occur for neurodivergent students

- effective adult communication strategies for communicating with a neurodiverse student population

- how to support students to express themselves

- how to create a communication-friendly environment in your setting.

THE COMMUNICATION PROCESS

Communication affects almost everything we do. Communication can be spoken, written, or (particularly using digital technologies) a combination of the two forms. Communication is a complex process and can be broken down into a number of steps:

Attention and listening

First of all we use our attention and listening skills to focus on what is being communicated. If we are listening, we need to be able to hear the words that are being said, eliminate distractions that are around us, focus on what is being said and maintain our concentration. If we are reading, we need to be able to see the text, ignore other distractions and sustain our attention on this.

Have you ever had to ask somebody to repeat something because you didn't hear them or there was too much background noise?

Or perhaps you have re-read the same page of text several times without really taking it in because your attention was wandering? These are examples of breakdowns in attention and listening.

Understanding

The next step is to understand what is being communicated. We need to understand individual words (vocabulary), as well as how sentences are constructed (grammar). In addition we need to understand any non-literal phrases (such as idioms, metaphors and common sayings) and to understand what is not said ('reading between the lines' or understanding the implied meaning). We also need to take into account the wider context and to consider what has already been said or discussed.

Processing

Understanding is closely linked to processing. We process the information that is communicated, making sense of it and linking it to what we already know. Memory also plays a role here as we need to remember what we have just heard or read.

Using language

Once we have listened to, understood and processed what we have heard, we may then wish to use language to respond. Using language involves several skills. We need to plan and prepare what we are going to say, thinking about the vocabulary and grammar we are going to use. When writing or giving an extended speech, we also need to consider the structure and organisation so that we can express our thoughts in a logical order which is easy to follow. Again, memory plays a role as we need to remember what we have already said and what we want to say next.

Social communication

When interacting with others, a number of other skills are also needed – social communication skills. These skills include understanding and using appropriate non-verbal communication (such as facial expression, eye contact, gesture and body language) and how we use our voice (changing our pace, intonation and tone, for example). Conversational skills also come into play: initiating, maintaining and ending conversations; changing topics appropriately; taking turns in conversation; using an appropriate level of formality and politeness and being relevant. More complex communication skills also come in here – such as using language for negotiation and compromise.

Students may have difficulties in one or several of these areas of communication.

COMMUNICATION IN SCHOOLS

To support a neurodiverse student population we need to consider how we communicate with students. Communication plays a huge role in school life. Just consider all of the various ways students are expected to communicate on a daily basis:

- Listening to the class teacher lead whole-class activities.

- Listening to adults leading small group activities.

- Contributing to whole class and small group activities.

- Working and talking on a one-to-one basis with teachers and other adults.

- Listening and participating in larger groups and gatherings such as assemblies.

- Asking for help when needed.

- Speaking and listening to other school staff such as receptionists, lunchtime supervisors and sports coaches.

- Talking with a partner or group of peers to complete work in class.

- Giving a presentation or talking in front of a group or class.

- Talking and playing with peers during social times.

- Negotiating, compromising and sorting out friendship difficulties.

- Passing on messages and information between home and school.

- Explaining an incident or difficulty to a member of staff.

- Explaining thoughts, feelings and worries to staff at home.

And that is to say nothing of all the written forms of communication which are expected during the day!

- Reading signs, posters and other information around school (behaviour rules, menus in the canteen, directions, etc.).

- Reading information and instructions displayed on the board.

- Reading worksheets, textbooks and other materials used in class.

- Reading test papers and examinations.

- Reading information from the internet and carrying out research.

- Making notes when listening or working.

- Copying information from the whiteboard or from books.

- Writing answers in exercise books.

- Writing or typing longer answers and essays.

- Producing work on the computer.

- Completing written tests and examinations.

- Completing written homework tasks.

- Noting down homework tasks and other reminders.

Language and communication really are at the very heart of learning. It is through language that we think and learn.

Remember that in any one class students may have differences in the way that they:

- attend and listen

- remain focused

- understand spoken language

- process spoken language

- understand and use vocabulary

- express themselves

- take part and follow conversation and discussion

- use and understand social communication skills

- process written information

- understand written information

- read and write

- produce structured and organised written work

- remember what has been said and read.

Misunderstandings and communication difficulties can often be at the root of many difficulties and problems which arise. In this chapter we consider adult communication strategies (for supporting expressive and receptive language) and communication-friendly environments. Ideas and strategies for supporting students with written work are included in Chapter 5, 'Teaching and Learning'.

ADULT COMMUNICATION STRATEGIES

Without realising it, adults can often communicate in a way which disadvantages neurodivergent students. There are, however, a number of strategies staff can use to support a greater proportion of the student population to understand, participate and express themselves.

The ideas that follow will support a larger proportion of the neurodiverse student population and will help many other students too. The suggestions are all positive habits to get into and will disadvantage no other student.

Please note: It is a common myth that only primary school children need support with their language and communication. In reality, we all continue to develop our communication skills throughout adolescence and beyond. All of the strategies that follow are equally, if not more, important to use in the secondary school classroom. Language and communication difficulties at this age may not appear so obvious at first. Many students can be struggling and hiding their difficulties. What on the surface may appear as 'poor behaviour' might in fact be arising due to difficulties with communication.

Supporting processing and understanding

Consider these points when talking to students in whole class, small group and individual situations.

Remove distractions

It is much harder to listen and understand if we are distracted by other things. Just think about the last time you struggled to pay attention in a meeting or lecture. Perhaps the room was too noisy or you were struggling to hear the speaker? Maybe you were physically uncomfortable or had something else on your mind? Remember that listening and understanding can be a chicken-and-egg type of problem. Students who are finding the content of a lesson difficult to understand are likely to be easily distracted. Equally, students who have difficulty paying attention are likely to struggle to understand as a result. The first thing we can do to help is to remove as many distractions in the environment as possible. Consider the following:

- **Background noise outside the classroom.** This may be outdoors or in the corridor. Some noise may be out of your control, but other sounds can be eliminated or reduced by closing doors, windows, blinds or through discussion and compromise with colleagues.

- **Background noise within the classroom.** Other adults and students talking or whispering can be very distracting.

Remember that background noise can appear amplified to some students with differences in the way that they process sensory information. Insist on silence when giving instructions and information to the whole class. Have quiet areas in the classroom, corridor or school library where students can work if they need a quieter environment to think. Have clearly defined acceptable noise levels when students are working.

- **Other background noise.** Sounds of noisy projectors, heating systems and computers can all be distracting. Turn off anything not in use.

- **Visual distractions outside the classroom.** A PE lesson taking place on the field or two students arguing in the corridor can be more interesting to some students than what is going on within the classroom! If these distractions cannot be removed, try closing blinds and consider seating plans. Arrange tables and chairs so that students are not directly facing the distractions.

- **Visual distractions within the classroom.** Audit your classroom for possible distractions. Turn off moving screensavers on computers not in use – movements such as these may distract some students and take their focus away from the learning. Monitor what other adults are doing when the teacher is talking. An adult tidying the classroom can also be more interesting to some students than listening to something they are finding difficult.

- **Technology.** Technology can be particularly distracting when students are meant to be listening. If students have PCs, laptops or tablets, ensure that screens are switched off during listening time. Although it has become second nature to many of us to be multitasking when using digital devices, plenty of research shows that this negatively affects our concentration and that it can, in fact, take several minutes for our brains to refocus fully on the original task (Kutscher 2016). Ensure you have students' full attention when giving instructions and information.

- **Furniture and equipment.** It can be hard to concentrate if you are working on a wobbly table or the legs on your chair are uneven. Fix issues such as these before they become a bigger issue. Consider also the order in which you do things. If you have just given back marked work, give students time to read this before expecting them to listen – otherwise attention is likely to be divided between listening to the new topic and thinking about the feedback they have just received.

- **Internal distractions.** Students may have difficulty concentrating if they are ruminating or worrying about something. Try to deal with any worries or concerns promptly so that students can focus on the task in hand. If it is not possible to solve a problem immediately, give the student a definite time and place when they can speak to you or another adult about the problem. Write down the appointment in their planner. This way they know they will definitely have the opportunity to talk through the problem with somebody later on.

Use names

Use the student's name before giving a direct instruction or question. This can help to focus their attention.

'Tom, could you give everybody a glue stick?'

is better than

'Could you give everybody a glue stick, ermm…Tom, can you do that for me?'

Increase wait time

Many students need additional processing time to make sense of what is being said. It can be tempting for adults in the classroom to expect answers instantaneously. Indeed, some research suggests that teachers only wait an average of one second before expecting a response (Stahl 1994). Try using the ten-second rule. When asking a question, wait up to ten seconds before expecting an answer. This can feel like an uncomfortably long time at first but it is the length of time that many students will need to process and understand information. Giving this extra time will help all students to think through their answers and to give more detailed, thoughtful responses.

Slow your pace

We all find it more difficult to understand speakers who talk too quickly or who do not pause frequently enough. Monitor your own speech and slow it down if you have a tendency to speak quickly. Get into the habit of pausing slightly after sentences and after key information. This will support students who need some extra time to think about what they are hearing.

Use visual support

Many students have difficulty understanding language for a variety of reasons. Help these students by using visual support to back up your language. This enables students to make sense of what they are hearing. It give them something to 'hang' the language on to. We have all experienced times when language alone makes little sense. As soon as we have a visual, however, we are able to understand better – just think of when you are following recipes, DIY instructions or if you are given lengthy verbal instructions without a map for support. Visual support in the classroom can include the following:

- Concrete objects
- Photographs
- Diagrams/flow charts
- Pictures/drawings/ symbols

- Video/animation
- Gesture/body language
- Drama/acting out/role play

Get into the habit of 'showing' students what to do rather than just telling. Act out instructions as you give them to support students who have difficulty understanding language. Show students exactly what you want them to do.

Make sure that any visual support you use is relevant. If choosing photos, pictures or videos, make sure that these reflect the objects you are using in class in order not to confuse students further.

Repeat then simplify

If a student does not appear to have understood, it can be tempting for us to immediately try to rephrase what we have said in an effort to help the student understand. However, if the language was at an appropriate level for the student, the problem may be that they simply need some additional time to make sense of what they have heard. By rephrasing we may, in fact, compound the problem by giving the student two different things to process. Allow at least ten seconds after speaking. If the student hasn't yet responded or indicated they have understood, repeat using the same language. If there is no response after your repetition, then try simplifying what you said.

Monitor your tone of voice

Some students can have difficulty understanding tone of voice, and others may have sensory sensitivities. Often a loud 'teaching voice' can be interpreted as being angry and shouting, which can cause distress to some students. Use a calm, neutral tone of voice when addressing students and try not to speak any louder than you need to. (This will benefit your voice too!) Some teachers use different strategies to get a class' attention, such as clapping, raising an arm or using a sound shaker such as a tambourine.

Give one instruction at a time

Giving too many instructions at once places a high demand on memory load. It can also be confusing and many students will remember only the first or last things that they have heard. Give just one or two instructions at a time. Consider this instruction:

> 'Right, I want you all to write your name and the date on the top of your paper, put your books on the pile on the side, leave your papers on my desk and tidy your pencils away. Then get your coats and drinks, take a snack if you want one, give me your dinner money if you have it and go out to play.'

Many students will hear only 'go out to play' or will remember to do just one or two of the things listed. Try instead:

> 'First can you all write your name and the date on the top of your paper.'

> (Pause while students carry out the task)

> 'Now can you put pencils back in the tubs.'

> (Pause)

> 'Now could you all put your books on the side and your papers here on my desk.'

> (Pause while students complete this)

> 'Does anybody have dinner money to give me?'

> (Pause)

> 'Now get your coats, drinks, snacks and go out to play.'

Give instructions in the right order

'Before' and 'after' can be difficult concepts for many children. Listen to this instruction:

'Before you put your books on my table I want you to stick your maps in. But before you do that, remember to write the title and date.'

For some students these concepts will be difficult to follow and they may not remember or understand which order you want them to do the instructions in, completing them instead in the order they were given, or just becoming confused and completing the first or last instruction. Try instead to use 'First...next...last' and give the instructions in the order they are to be carried out:

'First write the title and date. Next stick your map in. Then put your books on my table.'

Support the instruction with gestures and actions to show students what to do.

Say what you want, not what you don't want

Some students may not pick up on implied or inferred meaning. So, if you enter a room and say, 'It's very noisy in here', they might not realise that you are really implying that they need to be quieter. Equally, if you tell students what not to do, they might not understand what it is they need to be doing instead.

'Sit still and look at the demonstration' is better than 'Stop messing about.'

'Write down each calculation you have done' is better than 'Don't do the maths in your head.'

'Keep your feet still' is better than 'Stop kicking the chair in front.'

Explain new vocabulary

Lack of vocabulary knowledge can be a huge barrier to under-standing and to learning. It is not just topic-specific vocabulary that some students will struggle with but also general, everyday vocabulary. Students are expected to learn a huge number of new words every day in school – some of this vocabulary may be new and topic-specific (such as 'earthquake', 'epicentre', 'fault line', 'Richter scale'), and some may be previously learned vocabulary applied in a new context ('bank' used in terms of a 'river bank' rather than 'a place where you pay in money', or 'table' used as a 'set of figures displayed in columns' rather than 'a piece of furniture').

You should not avoid using more complex words, as it is important for students to encounter and use a wide range of vocabulary. However, be aware that many students will have difficulty understanding some of the words you use. Explain new vocabulary that you use and back this up with visual support. You could also try to include activities which reinforce or pre-teach key vocabulary which is coming up in your lessons. Vocabulary games can be easily incorporated into most subjects and lessons. (See the 'Teach, reinforce and revisit vocabulary' section of this chapter for more ideas.)

Beware metaphors, idioms and jokes

Some students will experience difficulty understanding figurative language such as metaphors and idioms. For some students, such as those on the autism spectrum, there will be a tendency to take language literally and other students, such as those with EAL or with a language-poor background, may not have come across these terms before. We use metaphors and idioms frequently, often without even realising. Just consider these common phrases:

'The long and the short of it is…'

'You've got your work cut out there…'

'Pigs might fly.'

'I was over the moon.'

Consider the idioms you tend to use in your own speech and, if you catch yourself using any, try to rephrase or explain them to your students. Cultivate an atmosphere in your classroom where students are encouraged to identify and ask about new words or phrases that they encounter.

Use fewer words

Have you ever spoken to or listened to somebody who simply uses too many words? Perhaps they spoke at length but actually said very little? Perhaps they were very wordy and they didn't get to the point? It is always more difficult to understand people who use too many words and this is especially true for students who have difficulty understanding and processing information. They will have difficulty in picking out the important points and ignoring what it not necessary. In addition, children with difficulties in paying attention and understanding are also more likely to 'switch off' and stop listening if they hear lots of words that aren't really telling them very much.

Again, monitor your own speech and don't use ten words where one word will do! Keep your language short and clear.

Check understanding effectively

When giving out instructions or information, it is useful to check students' understanding at regular intervals. This allows you to rectify any misunderstandings before students become too confused. However, it is important to check understanding effectively. Asking a closed question such as 'Do you understand?' is likely to invite a simple 'yes' or 'no' answer, and students will often say 'yes' to avoid further questioning or to avoid appearing as if they have not understood. Sometimes students are asked to repeat the instructions or information given, in order to check their understanding. Although this strategy requires more than simply a 'yes' or 'no' answer, you should be aware that some students may be repeating back the words that they have heard without actually understanding what they mean. When you check understanding, encourage students to use their own words to explain what they have understood. This can help to highlight any particular areas of difficulty.

'Amelia, what is the first thing you have to do?'

is better than

'Do you understand what you have to do?'

Eye contact

For some students, eye contact is extremely uncomfortable; they cannot maintain eye contact and listen simultaneously. They might not be looking but will be listening. Do not insist on eye contact if this is uncomfortable. Instead, suggest that students face your direction so that you know they are listening, even if they are looking down.

Remember that these strategies will support a wide range of students and will disadvantage nobody. Get into the habit of communicating in a more neurodiverse-friendly way. Some of these strategies may seem simple, but these small changes can make a big difference to some students.

TOP TIP! Students do not only communicate with class teachers. Ensure that all staff in a school – senior leaders, teachers, teaching assistants, lunchtime supervisors, receptionists, sports coaches – are aware of strategies that they can use to support communication with students.

Supporting students to use language

Students may not only need support to understand language but also to use language themselves. Some common difficulties for neurodivergent students (and many others) can include:

- giving one-word answers or talking in short sentences
- talking in long, rambling sentences which do not make sense
- structuring sentences
- being relevant
- remembering what they wanted to say
- using accurate vocabulary
- being anxious about speaking in front of others.

Try the following ideas to support students' expressive language when in a whole class, small group or one-to-one situation.

Give preparation time

Giving students a few moments to think about what they are going to say can be a simple way of supporting them to formulate and plan more detailed and relevant responses.

Allow verbal rehearsal

Try the 'Think, Pair, Share' strategy. Allow students a few moments to think about their response. Then give them a few minutes to discuss this with a partner. Finally, take feedback. This opportunity to verbally rehearse their answers with a partner will help some students to structure, organise and refine their thoughts. Verbal rehearsal with an adult can also work well.

Build in note-making time

Older students can benefit from being given time to make notes on what they want to add to the discussion. Remember that notes do not have to be full sentences, correctly spelled or punctuated. They can even be in the form of pictures and drawings. Provide some scrap paper or mini whiteboards for students to make brief notes. The act of note-taking can support students to think through what they want to say, and the notes themselves act as a reminder of their thoughts when it is time to speak or discuss – reducing memory load and the anxiety of forgetting.

Provide visual support

Visual support can also help students to include relevant information in their answers or to use specific vocabulary. A list of key words (with small visuals) can work well, as can providing a picture or photograph for support. Allow students to refer to these visual supports when planning their answers, when speaking and when writing.

Use sentence starters

Some students struggle to know how to start their sentences. Providing some relevant sentence starters for students to complete can help, and can also support students to give answers which stay on topic. Relevant sentence starters can easily be displayed on the board, wall or on prompt sheets. Ensure that you demonstrate how to use sentence starters and that students know to complete the sentences with more than one word.

'My favourite part of the story was…'

'I was most surprised when…'

'What I think will happen next is…'

Allow students to contribute in other ways

Some students experience significant anxiety about speaking in front of the class or a large group, so allow other ways for students to contribute while building up these skills slowly:

- Perhaps try allowing one person from each group or pair to feedback to the whole class, but ensure that all students have made a contribution to their group.

- Alternatively, you could ask students to move around the classroom to show if they agree or disagree with something (have a large 'agree' poster one side and a large 'disagree' poster the other) or to raise their hands to show agreement with various statements, so that they are still taking part.

- Older students with reasonable writing skills might like to take part in a 'silent debate'. Provide large pieces of paper for each group so that students can write down and respond to statements made by others, by using arrows, writing and even emoticons.

- Try to build in time to speak to quieter students on a one-to-one basis throughout the lesson so that they are still able to contribute their ideas.

- Giving a presentation to a small group may be less scary than to the whole class, or allow students to present with a partner or group.

Use something to back up the language

Some students may struggle to express themselves through language alone. It can be easier for some if they have something to back up the language they are using – perhaps a poster, model, chart or diagram. This can also help other students to understand what they are trying to say.

Teach higher-level language skills

Many students will need support in using language for more complex situations such as compromise, negotiation, agreement and disagreement.

Some students will need these skills taught explicitly. You might need to teach skills such as: polite ways of agreeing and disagreeing; how to negotiate; how to take turns; how to participate effectively in group discussion and group activities. You might try the following:

- Show a video or act out a role play of a poor example of these skills. Can students identify what was going wrong? What could the characters have done differently?

- Show a video or act out a role play of a more positive example of these skills. What was better about this? What were the characters doing that was effective?

- Provide some examples of useful sentence starters ('I only partly agree with Joe because…', 'I think that is a good point and I would add to it by saying…', 'Some people might argue with that point because…').

- Praise and point out these skills when you observe students using them.

- Use everyday teaching opportunities and activities to revisit these skills.

Teach, reinforce and revisit vocabulary

Vocabulary plays a big role in communication. There are many ways you can promote vocabulary knowledge in your everyday teaching. Why not try some of the following ideas:

- Have a 'Word Wall'. Display vocabulary with useful visuals related to the current topic that your class is studying. Refer to the wall regularly and encourage students to use the word to remind themselves of words (and to check spellings when doing written work).

- Write topic-specific vocabulary on small pieces of card and place in a 'Word Box'. Whenever there is a spare minute or two, pull out a word and generate discussion about it. Who can give a definition? Who can use it in a sentence?

- Provide lists of topic-specific words and pictures for students to refer to – these could be placed on tables or stuck into books. Send home lists so that students can refer to them when doing homework. Visual word lists can be created quickly in widget software such as Symwriter.

- Younger children could be set a 'talking homework'. Give parents a short list of topic-related vocabulary which the child has to tell them about.

- Build up an environment in your classroom where students are rewarded for identifying and asking about words that are unfamiliar to them. Facilitate discussion about the words that are identified.

- When giving students spellings to learn, ensure that you spend some time teaching the meanings too. Students often learn spellings without actually understanding the words they are spelling!

- Provide child-friendly dictionaries and thesauruses and promote the use of these across subjects and activities.

WORD GAMES THAT CAN BE ADAPTED FOR ANY SUBJECT

- **Taboo.** Place students in pairs or small teams. They have to take it in turns to describe topic-specific words (give a list to help) without using the word itself. How many can their partner/team guess correctly in two minutes?

- **Pictionary.** Use topic-specific words. One pupil draws a word and the others have to name it. Use this as an opportunity to reinforce what the word means.

- **Charades.** Again, use topic-specific words. This time the students act out the words for the others to guess.

- **Mind-mapping.** Ask teams of students to generate as many words as they can related to a topic.

- **Matching.** Match words to their definitions, or words with a visual.

- **Guess My Word.** 'I'm thinking of something that can be dormant or erupt.' Students can play in pairs or groups.

- **Twenty Questions.** One player thinks of a word and the others have to ask yes/no questions to guess the word within 20 questions. The original player can only answer 'yes' or 'no'.

COMMUNICATION-FRIENDLY ENVIRONMENTS

As well as considering how adults facilitate communication during the school day, we can also consider how 'communication-friendly' the physical environment is. Consider some of the following ideas:

Signs and posters

Much information is communicated via written means in educational institutions (safety rules, behaviour expectations, the lunch menu, etc.). Check that your written information meets the following criteria:

- It is displayed at students' eye-level. Posters that are too high or displayed behind doors will not be read so should be removed.

- It is written in child-friendly language. Use language and vocabulary which is suitable for the age group you work with. Language which is too complicated will not be read or understood; language which looks too 'babyish' will be ignored by older students.

- It has helpful and relevant visuals. Visuals can aid the processing and understanding of written language, so make sure that they are there for a purpose and are not misleading. A sign that says 'No eating', for example, should be illustrated by a picture of food with a cross through it, not just a picture of food, as this gives a conflicting message.

- It is not too wordy. Students will not bother to read long posters or lists of rules. Stick to the key points that students need to know.

- It is up to date. Old, out-of-date posters and signs will simply become background wallpaper – students will not see them as something which is important and needs to be read. Only display what is relevant.

- It is clear and uncrowded. Busy walls and display boards are unhelpful for communication. Many students will feel overwhelmed, will not know where to start and will not be able to pick out the key information. Stick to the key points and helpful visuals. Try not to overload display boards. Make it easy for students to see the key messages. Remember that 'less is more'.

- It is consistent. If you use symbols, pictures or colour coding, make these consistent across the setting.

Label resources and equipment

Supporting students to be able to locate resources and equipment easily also supports communication in the classroom, making it easier for students to respond to instructions, organise themselves and work independently. Try the following:

- Keep resources in clearly labelled trays, boxes, cupboards or drawers. Ensure that written labels are clear and supported by a visual of the resources or equipment they correspond to.

- Use consistent symbols or pictures around the school.

- Colour code or label exercise books to support organisation.

- Make frequently used resources easily accessible to students.

- Keep your classroom neat and tidy. Some students are easily distracted by too many things in the environment; others can be easily upset by lots of change in the environment or by too much clutter. Just think how you feel when the aisles in your favourite supermarket change or when you are trying to work in a cluttered environment!

Have clear signage around the school

As a professional who goes into many different schools, primary and secondary, I often find these places difficult to navigate. Finding toilets, classrooms, the staff room or my way back to reception can all be difficult tasks! Even when I do come across toilets, it can be unclear whether these are for staff or pupils. Imagine how difficult navigating the school environment can be for some students, especially those who have difficulties with direction, communication or memory! Even just being in the school environment can provoke anxiety. Many students find themselves following others to where they need to go or inadvertently get into trouble for being late or in the wrong place. Help students in the following ways:

- Have clear signs on doors to indicate what each room is used for. Make it clear if toilets are for staff or pupils.

- Use symbols or small pictures to back up the signs on each door.

- Include the staff name and photo on the door of each classroom – this helps students know if they are in the right place, and helps them to remember names!

- Have clear signage around the school, helping students (and visitors) to find their way.

- Use colour coding for each department, year group or key stage.

- Ensure signs are clear, consistent and stand out.

- Provide easy-to-read maps for students, particularly in larger schools.

COMMUNICATING FOR NEURODIVERSITY CHECKLIST

Do you:

☐ Remove visual, auditory, physical and technological distractions where possible?

☐ Use a student's name to ensure you have their attention?

☐ Wait at least ten seconds before expecting a response?

☐ Speak slowly and clearly, pausing to allow students to make sense of what they are hearing?

☐ Use visual support to back up instructions and information?

☐ Repeat when necessary and simplify language if appropriate?

☐ Use a calm, neutral and quiet tone of voice?

☐ Give instructions one at a time?

☐ Give instructions in the order they are to be carried out?

☐ Explain new vocabulary?

☐ Explain metaphors, idioms and other non-literal language?

☐ Use only as many words as necessary?

☐ Check understanding effectively?

☐ Give students time to prepare their answers?

☐ Give students time to rehearse verbally or to make notes?

☐ Provide visual and vocabulary support for students when answering, talking and discussing?

☐ Provide sentence starters for support?

☐ Allow students to contribute in other ways?

☐ Teach, reinforce and revisit new vocabulary at regular intervals?

In your classroom:

☐ Are resources and equipment clearly labelled with visual support?

☐ Are visuals and symbols used consistently across classrooms?

☐ Are resources and equipment kept tidy?

In the wider setting:

☐ Are rooms labelled clearly and consistently?

☐ Are rooms labelled with staff names and photos?

☐ Is there clear signage to support students to move around the school?

KEY POINTS

- Language and communication are at the very heart of learning; it is through language that we think and learn. Many students have different ways of communicating.

- There are many small changes that adults can make to their own language which will help students to understand and process information. These strategies work best if all adults use them. Students not only communicate with teachers but also with teaching assistants, receptionists, sports coaches and lunchtime supervisors, to name just a few.

- Giving students extra time to process information and to formulate their responses can help many. Having an added emphasis on teaching vocabulary will also support a wide range of students.

- It is not only in the classroom that students may struggle to communicate. Some may also have difficulty in recounting events or incidents and in expressing their thoughts and feelings. Use these strategies across situations.

• The physical environment around us can also make it easier or harder for some students to communicate. Audit your environment and check that you are not misguiding students or increasing their difficulties.

4

GETTING THE ENVIRONMENT RIGHT

In this chapter you will learn:

- how the physical environment can help or hinder a neurodiverse student population

- how you can ensure that classrooms, and shared spaces around the school, are inclusive

- how to ensure the teaching materials, classroom resources and equipment support the wide range of students in each class.

THE PHYSICAL ENVIRONMENT

The environment around us can have a considerable impact on our wellbeing, as well as on our ability to learn and concentrate. Busy school environments have often been designed for only one way of neurocognitive functioning (the 'neurotypical' style), which can make it harder for those who function differently.

- Those who process sensory information differently can be overwhelmed by too much sensory input, causing increased anxiety and an impaired ability to focus. Sensory input can include noise, sights/visuals, smells, tastes, textures, movement and people.

- Students who have differences with motor skills, spatial awareness or balance may find equipment and the physical environment difficult to navigate, causing frustration and low self-esteem.

- Those who relate to others differently may have difficulty with some expected parts of the school day, such as social times or group work.

IN THE CLASSROOM

What can we do to make the classroom more comfortable for a larger proportion of the neurodiverse student population?

- Ensure tables and chairs are the right height for students.

- Leave enough space around tables for students to walk freely without bumping into others' tables and chairs.

- When talking to students, try not to stand too close or to lean over their shoulders. This close physical proximity can feel uncomfortable for some.

- Consider your seating plan:

  ° Do students have enough space around them? (Physical proximity can be overwhelming and uncomfortable for some.)

  ° Are all students seated where they can easily see the teacher and board without having to turn around frequently?

  ° Are left-handers and right-handers placed so that their writing arms are not adjacent and bumping as they write?

  ° Do students have sufficient space on their desks and a neat, clutter-free workspace?

- Check the lighting. Artificial fluorescent lighting is uncomfortable for many. Allow natural lighting when possible and turn off the lights when they are not necessary.

Dim lights when possible, especially when displaying information on the screen to ensure there is not too much glare on the board.

- Keep your classroom tidy and clutter free. Keep resources in set places, clearly labelled. Avoid having piles of things on the floor or furniture that juts out.

- Audit your displays. 'Busy' visuals of many colours can be overwhelming for many students. There can often be the temptation to 'overdecorate' classrooms with wall, ceiling, door and window displays. This can be distracting for many students and can lessen the impact of the displays. Keep displays neat and simple.

- Allow movement breaks and opportunities for students to get up and stretch. Sitting in one position for too long can be uncomfortable.

- Some students can have difficulty in holding their body upwards and straight. Sitting on the carpet might be difficult and you might see them leaning against furniture or other pupils to help them 'feel' where their body is in space. Allow pupils to sit on chairs or to sit against a wall.

- Provide quiet spaces to work. Some students can feel extremely anxious being around other people, and small noises such as breathing or pen-tapping can appear amplified. These pupils can concentrate more effectively when working alone. Ensure that there are quieter spaces available for students to work in. Make these available for any students who would like to use them. This reduces any stigma attached and makes it a normal part of everyday classroom practice.

NON-ACADEMIC LESSONS

It is not only in the traditional 'classroom' lessons that some students can experience difficulty. Subjects such as PE, technology, art, music and outdoor education can all bring their own challenges for some neurodivergent students due to the comparative lack of structure, emphasis on teamwork or physical expectations. How can you help?

- Provide easy-to-use equipment and spend time teaching students how to use these tools effectively. Knives, tin-openers, spanners – all can be difficult for some students, so set aside time for students to learn and practise how to manipulate these items.

- Allocate additional time for tasks that require motor skills. Many students can find cutting, sticking or using tools difficult. This can become even more anxiety provoking when feeling under the pressure of time constraints.

- Ensure there is enough space to complete physical tasks.

- Be aware that smells and tastes can be difficult for some students to filter out when in cooking or technology classrooms. The noise of music classrooms can also be uncomfortable, so allow students to practise in quieter areas when possible.

- Bring structure to the less structured. When working outside or in other environments, remember that students will still benefit from being told the structure of the lesson so that they know what is coming up and in which order. Flipcharts or large pieces of paper can be easy to move to different areas.

- Remember too, that the same strategies for adult communication are relevant whatever environment you are working in. See Chapter 3, 'Communication', for more detail.

- Group work can also induce anxiety in some students. See Chapter 5, 'Teaching and Learning', for helpful strategies.

Physical education (PE)

PE lessons can often be a source of stress and frustration for some neurodivergent students, particularly those with motor, sensory or social differences. Just imagine the following scenario:

Sarah has just two minutes to get changed for her PE lesson. She has difficulties with motor skills so finds she fumbles with her shoelaces, zips and buttons. Despite staying on task and changing as quickly as she can, she is still the last in the changing room. Her teacher shouts to her to hurry up. This makes her panic and it takes her even longer to finish getting changed. She arrives late to the rest of the group, who have already been told what they are doing that lesson. She is then picked last for a team as others know she is not great at sport. Sarah finds catching and throwing a ball difficult and also does not know where to place herself in the game of netball. She doesn't like to get too close to other people as she feels she is invading their space. Nobody throws the ball to her and when they do she drops it, to groans and shouts of disappointment from her teammates. She doesn't quite understand the rules of netball and finds the game hard to keep up with; everything seems to move so quickly. She can't listen to her teammates and move at the same time. Other people push her out of the way and she bumps into others. At the end of the lesson she is again last to get changed, meaning she is late for her next lesson and gets a detention. She feels sticky and uncomfortable for the rest of the day and finds it hard to concentrate.

Supporting PE lessons:

- Allocate extra time for getting changed; not all students can do this quickly.

- Suggest PE kit which is soft, comfortable and easy to get on. Velcro trainers, for example, can be quicker to put on than ones with laces.

- Ensure that staff allocate teams or groups.

- Remember that team games are not for everyone and might put some students off exercise for good. Provide a mix of team and individual activities.

- Explain rules clearly and in several ways – not just through language. Do demonstrations or show diagrams or videos.

- Some students will find skills such as catching, throwing or kicking balls very difficult. Provide time for them to practise with supportive peers.

- See also the section 'Group work' in Chapter 5.

SHARED SPACES

Shared spaces around school are often forgotten but can be just as difficult to navigate as the classroom itself.

Navigating the school

Corridors and open shared spaces can present specific difficulties. With space at a premium in many schools, it can be easy for these areas to become cluttered, crowded and used for multiple purposes.

- Define the use of each space. Create different 'zones' through colour-coding, clear signs and helpful visuals. Furniture or display boards can also be positioned to create specific areas such as a cloakroom or silent reading area.

- Use natural lighting where possible. It can become a habit to turn lights on when they are not needed – some pupils can be particularly distressed by fluorescent lighting.

- Low tables and storage boxes can be difficult for children with poor spatial awareness – keep furniture against the wall to prevent trips and bumps.

- Brightly coloured walls brimming with work and posters are a feature of many schools but can be overwhelming to some pupils. Keep displays tidy, relevant and use neutral background colours.

- Narrow corridors can induce anxiety in pupils who are uncomfortable in groups of people. Dismiss one group of pupils at a time or introduce a one-way system.

Assemblies and larger gatherings

Larger gatherings can also create anxiety for some pupils. Some children may feel more comfortable at the end of a row or near the back rather than at the centre of a crowd of people. Others may find it difficult to know how close or far away to sit from other pupils. You could try using masking tape to indicate the distance needed between one row of pupils and another, or have a clear rule (one pupil per carpet tile, for example). Visuals can also be helpful to give all pupils some clear guidelines (e.g. when queueing, the person in front should be an arm's length away). Space out rows of chairs so that pupils do not feel squashed.

Remember too that some pupils may be particularly sensitive to noise. If a video or music is playing, they might be more comfortable sitting further from the stage or away from speakers.

Social times

Break and lunch times are often cited as a time of difficulty for some students, often due to the lack of structure and the emphasis on socialising.

- Structured activities and games led by an adult may help some pupils understand how to participate.

- Create a space (indoors or on the playground) for arts, crafts and toys. This allows pupils to engage in an individual activity while still being in the company of others – reducing feelings of isolation and loneliness while removing the anxiety of having to interact.

- Buddy benches may also be beneficial – provide a bench where any child can sit when they would like to join in or are feeling lonely. Other pupils are encouraged to keep an eye out and help those sitting on the bench to join in.

- Clear zones can be helpful on the playground. Signpost which are areas for running, ball games, toys or other activities.

- Some students will need to spend social times alone – the social interaction of lessons can be enough for them and they will need alone time in order to 'recover'. Provide quiet spaces which are *kept* quiet and peaceful. Allowing any pupil to make use of these when they need to will reduce any stigma attached.

- Dining halls can be especially difficult due to the mass of smells, people, noises, tastes, textures and movement. A child with heightened senses might be able to hear every crunch and every rustle of a crisp packet as loudly as their own! Clear dining hall routines for lining up and eating can be helpful, as can providing quieter areas.

MATERIALS, RESOURCES AND EQUIPMENT

Our classrooms tend to be full of materials, resources and equipment – textbooks, exercise books, pencils, science apparatus, calculators, books, art materials, musical instruments, posters, worksheets, computers, tablets, whiteboards, rulers, crayons. Very few activities in the classroom take place without using any materials and resources at all. These resources we use can again sometimes disadvantage some students – many have been designed for just one type of neurocognitive learning style. There are other resources which can be incredibly helpful for some students but are not often used due to a lack of awareness, funding, or sometimes the belief that students should not appear different to others. In this section we will consider helpful resources to have in all classrooms and how to adapt resources to make them more suitable for a wider proportion of students.

Useful resources for all classrooms

In the twenty-first century we are lucky that there are many helpful resources available which have been designed to support neurodivergent students in the classroom. These range from pencil grips and coloured overlays to computer software and apps. However, despite the existence of these, they are not always used, or often only used too late after a student has been struggling and has experienced considerable difficulty and failure. A specialist may then become involved and suggest certain equipment or materials are used. Some comments often heard are:

'Yes, we know the dyslexic students would benefit from using laptops and voice-text software, but they don't like appearing different in the classroom. It makes them stand out so we don't use it.' (Secondary school SENCO)

'We got a pencil grip for the child, but he lost it and we don't have an unlimited budget.' (Primary class teacher)

'We do have a writing slope somewhere. Perhaps it is in the store cupboard. We've tidied it away.' (Primary school SENCO)

'We have screenreading technology on all the computers, but pupils don't use it. I don't know if they know it is there.' (Secondary inclusion leader)

The problem in many schools is that many useful resources are not made available to pupils. They not seen as an important enough investment, or students are not taught to use them effectively. In addition, some students (and teachers) see using additional resources to be out of the ordinary or in some way different. However, with an increasingly neurodiverse student body, it is important that schools move away from this approach. Some very simple additional resources can make a huge difference to some students – helping them to participate, to achieve and to increase their self-esteem. Students should not be made to feel any 'different' for using certain resources or equipment; instead, this should become a normal part of everyday classroom practice. Making resources and equipment available to all students from the very beginning removes any stigma attached to these things. Let's look now at some resources which are useful in every classroom and how they can help.

Pencil grips

Pencil grips are usually made from rubber and come in a variety of shapes and sizes. They can be placed on most standard-sized pens and pencils. A pencil grip can improve some children's ability to grip a pencil and to write comfortably. These may also have a positive impact on the standard of handwriting a child produces and the amount they can produce. Pencil grips can also support some children to learn where to grip the pencil and the most effective angle to hold the pencil.

Writing slopes

A writing slope is a wedge-shaped slope which is placed on the desk. Some students find it easier to write using the slope, compared to on a flat desk. It can help to make writing more comfortable and can improve the quality of handwriting.

Coloured overlays

Coloured overlays are transparent plastic overlays (some come in the form of rulers) which students can place over a book or worksheet to help them to read. These can be particularly useful for students who experience visual stress when reading or some types of dyslexia. For some students, reading black text on white paper can be too much of a contrast and can impede their ability to read. Students with visual stress will need a specialist assessment to ascertain which colour overlay benefits them the most. Some may be prescribed tinted lenses in their glasses rather than, or as well as, using coloured overlays. However, having a range of overlays available for everybody in the classroom from the beginning can be beneficial. Some students may find out which colour works for them from a process of trial and error – this can be useful information for them to take to an assessment. Others may not have a formal diagnosis but find it more comfortable to read with an overlay – this should be encouraged.

Wobble cushions/wedge cushions

Wobble cushions can help some children to sit still and feel more comfortable on their chairs. Wedge cushions can help some children with their sitting posture, encouraging them to sit at a more comfortable angle and position.

The importance of having the right-sized tables and chairs should also not be underestimated. Have you ever spent an uncomfortable day working at a table or chair that was the wrong size for you? Perhaps you felt as though you were having to slouch forward or that your arms were too high? Perhaps your knees were squashed uncomfortably under the desk. All of these things can affect children too, and the reasons for their fidgeting, movement and untidy work presentation may sometimes be down to something as simple as sitting at the wrong-sized table or chairs. This may be a particular problem for children who are tall or short for their age, as well as those with physical or motor difficulties.

Fiddle toys

Fiddle toys help some students to concentrate when they are listening. They can be useful as they provide something appropriate to fiddle with, rather than classroom resources and apparatus which could easily be broken. They come in a range of shapes and sizes. It is important to remember that fiddle toys are designed to improve concentration and not to be an additional distraction! They are best used discreetly, under the table, perhaps, and they should help the student to concentrate on the lesson content; their attention should not be focused on the toy to the exclusion of everything else. Choose fiddle toys which are not easily broken and which allow hand movement without requiring too much attention.

Dictionaries

There are many child-friendly dictionaries available, the best including diagrams and pictures as well as word definitions. Some dictionaries are also arranged semantically (by topic) and others are arranged phonetically rather than alphabetically. This means that words are arranged by the sounds, rather than just the letters, and this can be particularly useful for students who are finding spelling difficult. The word 'psychology', for example, would be placed under 's' as well as 'p'. The word 'phantom' would be found under both 'ph' and 'f'. Encourage students to get into good habits of using dictionaries whenever possible. Make them easily accessible in all subjects, not only English lessons. They can be invaluable in supporting students with both word meanings and spellings. Remember that many students will need to be taught how to use a dictionary effectively. Providing an alphabet arc in the classroom or in books can also support those young people who have difficulty in remembering alphabetical order.

Number lines/number squares

Providing number lines or a number square can also benefit many students and not just in maths lessons. Number work comes up across the curriculum – in science, technology, geography and cooking, for example. Numbers are also often referred to in many other subjects and contexts. We might, for example, mention percentages or fractions, or ask students to count. Having number lines and number squares available across the curriculum can help to reduce anxiety in students who find number work difficult.

Spellcheckers

Electronic spellcheckers can also be a way of supporting students to check spellings and word meanings independently. Many read the words and definitions aloud, supporting those who have difficulty decoding the words.

Vocabulary lists

Providing a list of key vocabulary can be helpful for all age groups and subjects. Add small pictures or symbols to the topic-specific vocabulary list to aid understanding. Students may each be provided with a copy of the list, or it may be displayed on the wall, or both. Having this visual reminder can help students understand words when they hear or read them; it can remind them to use these words in their own talking and writing; it can also act as a spelling aid for those who have difficulty remembering spellings.

Small whiteboards or paper notepads

It may sound easy but simply having small wipe-clean whiteboards or some scrap paper available can be helpful in many ways. Some students benefit from noting down key words, numbers or concepts as they are listening, to act as a memory aid. Others may like to try out various spellings before deciding which version 'looks' right. This can increase confidence in poor spellers who are anxious about getting the correct spelling in their work. As adults, we do these things all of the time without even noticing – we make a rough outline of the points we want to make in an email, we note down a key word or a number to remind us of something, we try out spellings, we note down a name we might forget. Encourage students to get into the habit of noting down anything they need to. It's a simple strategy but can be helpful for many.

There are also many useful resources which can support students with their reading, writing and mathematics. For more detail on these, see Chapter 5, 'Teaching and Learning'. Resources and equipment which can support memory and independence are also listed in Chapter 5.

TOP TIP! To reduce any stigma or uncertainty students may have about using these resources, have them available from the beginning of the year and make them available to all students. They should become part of everyday classroom practice. Remind all students frequently that these things are available for anybody who finds them helpful and teach students how to use them. Reinforce the fact that everybody is different and will find different things helpful.

What if students use these things and don't need them? It is likely that, at first, many students will want to try out new resources and equipment – that is great! It shows to students who do need them that these things are interesting and credible. The resources listed above are also not going to harm any student who does not need them. What is likely to happen is that the novelty of using something new will wear off after a while for those who not do see any benefit in using them, while those who are helped will continue using them. In the meantime many students have been helped and an atmosphere of inclusion and acceptance has been reinforced.

Ensuring teaching and learning materials do not disadvantage

As well as providing helpful resources within the classroom, we can also ensure that any existing teaching and learning materials do not disadvantage neurodivergent students. Often some small tweaks are all that is needed to create more inclusive materials, and these small changes can make a big difference. Some examples are given below.

Displaying teaching materials on the board

Whole class teaching is often led by displaying a presentation on the interactive whiteboard, but this can be difficult for some students to read. Consider the following points:

- What background colour have you used? The contrast of black text on a white background can be too strong for some students, making the screen 'glare'. Try using a pale pastel colour for the background instead to reduce the contrast. Beware too of patterned or colourful backgrounds, which can make text hard to read and can be distracting. Avoid using green or red text as this can be difficult to read for individuals who are colour blind.

- Which font have you used? Some fonts can be easier to read than others, particularly for students who have dyslexia or visual difficulties. Use a plain, clear sans serif font such as Arial, Verdana, Tahoma, Calibri, Century Gothic, Comic Sans or Trebuchet (BDA 2017). Check that the font does not run letters together. Some fonts can, for example, make 'r n' look like 'm', so the word 'modern' could be read as 'modem'. Small things like this can make a text difficult to comprehend, so find an easy-to-read font and get into the habit of using it. It only takes a second to change the font of an entire presentation or document.

- Is text well spaced? Use a font size which can be easily read by students at the back of the classroom. Make sure that there are clear spaces between words and lines. Change the 'line spacing' on your document if you need to.

- Is text easy to read? <u>Underlining</u> and *using italics* can make some fonts appear as if the letters are merging into each other. Use **bold** instead to make words stand out. Avoid using text in BLOCK CAPITALS as this can also be more difficult to read (BDA 2017).

- Are visuals helpful rather than distracting? Images which move, flicker or fly in can all be distracting to some students. Other students may be relying on the images to help them to understand the written text, so make sure that any pictures are helpful and relevant rather than confusing. Try not to be tempted to include images just to 'brighten up' slides.

- Is there too much information? Some students find it difficult to focus on the important information and to ignore what is not relevant. Ensure that you keep to the important points and remove any pictures, patterns or other information which is unnecessary. Some students may also be overwhelmed by too much information at once. Display just one piece of information at a time to improve focus and to reduce frustration.

Producing typed materials such as worksheets

Similar strategies are also relevant when producing typed materials such as worksheets or photocopiable resources.

- Use a clear sans serif font.

- Print materials onto a cream or pastel-coloured paper.

- Use font size 12 or 14 for ease of reading.

- Use line spacing of at least 1.5.

- Use bold text rather than underlining, italics and block capitals.

- Have clear spaces between paragraphs and boxes.

- Use left-justified text with a right ragged edge as this is easier to read. Justifying text leaves inconsistent spaces between letters and words, which can make it harder to read.

- Avoid narrow columns (like in newspapers).

- Remove unhelpful pictures and distractions. Ensure any visuals are relevant and aid understanding.

Many students have difficulty in understanding language, as we learned in Chapter 3, 'Communication'. These difficulties will extend to written language too, so when creating worksheets or presentations:

- use vocabulary which is age-appropriate and explain any difficult words

- use clear, simple sentences where possible

- use the active rather than the passive voice ('The dog bit the man' is easier to understand than 'The man was bitten by the dog')

- use helpful visuals, pictures, diagrams or flow charts to aid understanding

- use bullet points or numbered lists

- avoid double negatives

- explain any idioms, metaphors or non-literal language

- have key information in a box or bold text.

TOP TIP! Get into the habit of making these small changes. Soon it will become second nature and, again, these strategies do not disadvantage any other student.

AN ENVIRONMENT FOR NEURODIVERSITY AUDIT

Do you:

☐ Have furniture which is the right height?

☐ Ensure there is space to move around the classroom freely?

☐ Consider the seating plan so that students can all see what is going on?

☐ Use natural lighting whenever possible?

☐ Reduce or eliminate background noise?

☐ Allow movement breaks?

☐ Keep your displays neat, tidy and relevant?

☐ Provide quiet areas for work, which are kept quiet?

☐ Allow additional time for tasks requiring motor control?

☐ Provide useful resources and learning materials in your classroom for all students to make use of?

☐ Ensure that written information on the board is clearly displayed?

☐ Produce easy-to-read written information such as worksheets?

☐ Keep resources and materials tidy and clearly labelled?

☐ Keep corridors and shared areas clutter-free?

☐ Have clear and consistent routines for social times?

☐ Have quiet areas for break and lunch times, which are kept quiet?

☐ Provide a range of structured activities for students to engage with at social times?

☐ Have clearly designated zones for different activities and have clear signage around the school?

KEY POINTS

- There are many helpful resources available which can help some students to achieve and participate in class. Have these available from the beginning of the year and make them available to all students. This will help to reduce any stigma attached to using something different and will also help students from the start rather than waiting until a problem develops.

- Some small tweaks can be made to teaching materials to prevent some students from being put at a disadvantage. Consider the presentations and written documents that are provided and how these can be adapted to meet the needs of a wider proportion of students.

- The physical environment also plays a role in how students are able to learn. Neurodivergent students may be particularly sensitive to sensory input.

- It is not only in the classroom that students can experience difficulties. Shared spaces and practical subjects can also be difficult for students to navigate.

5

TEACHING AND LEARNING

In this chapter you will learn:

- how to support students who have differences in the way they acquire reading, writing and mathematics across the curriculum
- how to support group work in the classroom
- how to develop independence and organisation in students
- how to support memory load in the classroom situation.

We have now looked at what can be done on a whole school level to support a neurodiverse student population and have considered how we can adapt the environment and adult communication styles in order to enable neurodivergent students to flourish. This chapter looks more specifically at what can be done in the classroom to support teaching and learning. The strategies are suitable for both primary and secondary schools when used in an age-appropriate manner and, as with all the previous chapters, they are most effective when used consistently across all lessons and staff.

READING

Students can have difficulties with reading for many reasons. Some students may have difficulty in decoding the actual letters but have good understanding. Others may be able to decode well but have little understanding of what they are reading. Some might have difficulty with both aspects. Others may find it difficult to remember what they have read, to keep track of longer texts or to pick up on the inferred information.

> **TOP TIP!** It is not just the responsibility of English teachers to support students who have difficulty reading. Although a set member of staff may be given the responsibility of delivering a reading intervention or catch-up, all staff need to be aware of how they can support students with reading difficulties. Every subject requires some reading – whether it is reading questions, instructions, source material, textbooks or websites. The strategies below are for staff to use across the curriculum so that reading difficulties do not become a barrier to students achieving in other subjects.

Teaching strategies to support reading difficulties

So what can you do to support students with reading difficulties across the curriculum?

- Get into the habit of producing written materials (presentations and worksheets) which are clear and easy to read. See the section 'Materials, resources and equipment' in Chapter 4 for a more detailed checklist. Use a clear font, space out information clearly, use straightforward language and make sure any visuals are helpful and relevant.

- Give students sufficient time to complete any activities that involve reading information which is on the board or in front of them. Some students will need considerable time to decode and make sense of the information, so take this into account before moving on to the next activity.

- Read aloud printed instructions and information to the whole class. Get into the habit of reading out loud what is on your presentation slides and reading out the questions or instructions on any worksheets. This is also a good opportunity to check understanding.

- Remind students that it is ok for them to put their hand up and ask for help with reading the questions or instructions as they are working. Cultivate an 'it's OK to ask for help' atmosphere in your classroom.

- Encourage students to identify and ask about the meaning of any words that are new to them. This additional emphasis on vocabulary will help all students. Make it an expected part of classroom practice for students to ask about new words they encounter. Word games are easily built into many everyday classroom activities.

- When working on a text, encourage students to highlight key words, underline key phrases or annotate with notes or small pictures. This can help students to find the important information when they come to answering questions or using the text to revise from.

- Students working independently doing research on the internet can be shown how to use screenreading technology if they find this helpful. Screenreaders are built into most computers and digital devices. The text onscreen is read aloud. In Windows the screen-reader facility is called 'Narrator'. Students will need a small pair of headphones and will need to be shown how to change the voice to the one they find easiest to listen to and to change the speed of the voice to a pace they find most comfortable. Screenreaders can be very useful for those students who have good understanding but weak decoding. Be aware, however, that some students may not find spoken language any easier to understand than written language.

- Reading pens can also be beneficial to some students. These can be used to read aloud words in printed texts that a student is unable to read.

- Help students to understand written materials by creating opportunity to discuss them. This can be done on a whole class level, small group level or with a partner. Students could be given a few minutes to ask their partner questions about what they have read. This can enable them to gain clarification on points that they might not have understood themselves.

- Use visual back-up to support understanding. If you are working on a text which explains a process or event, see if you can find a picture, flow chart, diagram or video to aid understanding. If you are working on a fictional text you could try acting out the events of the story to help students who have had difficulty understanding.

- Making a cartoon strip of the events of the story can also be beneficial. This can be an opportunity to reinforce what has happened as well as discussing characters' feelings and motives.

- Encourage older students to take notes as they are reading to help them remember the information. Remind them that notes can be single words or even small diagrams and symbols.

- Use a folded piece of paper as a bookmark or a small wipe-clean bookmark. Ask students to note down the key points after each reading session. This can help them to make sense of what they have just read and to reinforce their learning. The bookmark can then be used before the next reading session to refresh their memory about what they read.

- And, finally, try to ensure that any reading materials you use are at the right reading age for your students. Materials taken straight from the internet are likely to be aimed at adults and will be difficult for many students to understand. Gather your materials from sources which have been written for the reading age of your students.

WRITING

Students may also have a range of writing difficulties. For some the difficulties may be physical (motor), meaning they find it difficult to grasp a pen and co-ordinate their movements. Some may have visual or spatial difficulties, meaning they find it hard to form letters accurately or to space out their work. Others may have difficulty with acquiring spelling knowledge, and others may find it hard to structure sentences correctly, to use appropriate grammar and punctuation or to know how to structure and organise a longer piece of writing so that it flows and expresses their thoughts in a logical sequence. As with reading, writing is not just the responsibility of English teachers but affects students across the curriculum. All teachers need to be aware of how they can support writing.

Supporting writing

- Mark for content rather than presentation. Give feedback on what students have included in their answers, rather than the state of their handwriting – most students will already know that they do not have neat handwriting, so being reminded of this often will only lower their self-esteem further.

- Give sufficient time for writing tasks. Some students need longer than others for either the physical process of handwriting or for them to process, order and structure their thoughts. Give feedback on quality rather than quantity.

- Make available resources such as pencil grips and writing slopes – these can make the writing process more comfortable for some students.

- Don't let spelling be a barrier to students showing what they know. Some students are embarrassed about their spelling and avoid writing tasks because of it. Other students find that they do not get much written work done because they are spending so long worrying about the spellings they are using. Make dictionaries or electronic spellcheckers available and encourage students to use these to check spellings. Provide a list of topic-specific vocabulary for students to refer to when they are writing to save them time asking about and looking up spellings.

- Build in time for students to proofread their work. Just a few moments reading through their work once finished can help some students to identify spelling errors or sentences that do not make sense. Students who have typed work could listen back to it being read out by screenreading technology; they might be better able to identify their errors this way.

- Provide sentence starters for students who are unsure how to begin a sentence. Over time, this will show them appropriate ways of beginning sentences and some may then begin to be able to use these independently.

- Create time for verbal rehearsal. Some students are able to write clearer sentences if they have had an opportunity to say them aloud first. Some students may benefit from saying their sentences to a partner or adult before writing them down.

- Talk before you write. Beginning a piece of writing on a blank page can be a scary task. All students can benefit from discussing their writing before they put pen to paper. Discuss the task and what they want to include in their answer.

- Providing prompts such as pictures, photos or diagrams can help some students to think of what to write.

- Use planning frames and storyboards to support the planning process. Students can plan what they want to include in each paragraph before writing the final piece. Make sure students refer to their planning sheet during the writing process. Post-it® notes can also be a way of generating ideas and moving them around on the page to structure a piece of writing.

- Allow other ways of recording. In most subjects handwriting is not the main concern, so do not let this be a barrier to students demonstrating knowledge. If students can type quickly, allow them to use a computer to produce written work. Make sure that students are taught touch-typing skills and that they do not have access to computer games or the internet when writing, as these can be a distraction. Some students might like to use voice-text software. Students speak into a microphone or their device and the software transforms their speech into typed text. Students will then just need to read back the text to add punctuation and to check that words have been recorded correctly. Using alternative methods of recording can also help students to take more pride in their work if they find it difficult to produce neat written work.

It's not all about literacy

The myth perhaps survives that students are only learning if they are reading and writing, but this is far from the case. We often mainly learn by doing practical activities, through discussion and through engaging with feedback on our performance. We also learn through watching, asking questions and experimenting with new ways of doing things. Reading is just one way of taking in information, and writing is just one way of demonstrating our knowledge.

Many education systems, however, are weighted heavily towards these styles of learning, which may not be the best for every student. Consider your teaching style and whether you create sufficient opportunities for students to learn in different ways, such as:

- researching and taking part in an oral debate

- researching and giving an oral presentation, taking questions from the audience

- listening to TED talks or attending talks related to the curriculum

- discussion with a partner or a group

- taking part in role play or drama activities

- providing learning games

- making models and prototypes

- teaching others in the class

- carrying out experiments

- summarising their learning in a drawing, diagram or flow chart

- submitting an audio file instead of a written essay

- making a video or news report

- annotating photos of them carrying out a practical task.

MATHS

Maths is also often thought of as the job of the maths teacher, but number work also affects most of the curriculum. Just think of the following examples:

- **Science.** The counting, measuring and weighing of chemical solutions and materials, the timing of tasks, displaying results in a chart or table, reading graphs, using and understanding formulas, using fractions and decimals.

- **Geography.** Understanding distances and scales on maps, understanding directions.

- **History**. Understanding dates and timelines.

- **PE**. Keeping the score in games, measuring heights and distances in athletics, understanding football league tables, timing races.

- **Cooking**.Weighing and measuring ingredients, doubling or halving ingredients to make a smaller or larger batch, using timers, understanding calories.

- **Technology**. Measuring and weighing equipment, drawing to scale, using formulas.

- **Foreign languages**. Learning how to count, tell the time and use money in a foreign language.

And this is to say nothing of just getting through everyday life. Number and maths work is used on a daily basis for:

- reading and following timetables

- telling the time – knowing what time to be at what place

- understanding the passage of time (so if somebody says, 'Come back in ten minutes' or 'You have 20 minutes for this task', how long is that?)

- using money to pay for lunch, equipment or school trips

- counting (e.g. when playing hide and seek)

- talking about the future (e.g. 'Next May you have an exam').

There are many students who have not yet secured some basic skills (such as sequencing the months of the year, using money or telling the time) and as a result school can be a confusing place. Older students in particular may be unwilling to admit that they find these skills difficult. So what can you do to support students?

- Use timelines to support students with their understanding of dates and the order of events. Timelines can be made easily and can cover a longer period (to order historical events, for example) or a shorter time frame (the events in a story, the events of the next academic year).

• Show students how to use calendars and diaries. It is not enough simply to give students timetables, a calendar or a diary; many will also need to be taught explicitly how to use these. If you have a calendar or a weekly planner on the wall, refer to it frequently to make use of it and to show students how to use it independently.

• When mentioning upcoming activities or events, refer to a calendar or diary to help students to understand (e.g. 'We have an exam coming up in December. Look in your diaries. That is three weeks away. So you have this week, another week and then the week after is your exam').

• Use sand timers or other visual timers (many are available electronically and can easily be displayed on a screen) to show the length of time students have to spend on a task. Students can then 'see' the amount of time remaining even if they struggle to tell the time.

• Provide number lines and number squares for students to refer to – some may struggle to understand which numbers are larger/smaller without these. These can also help students to count or to understand timings (e.g. if they have put something in the oven for 20 minutes and see that 18 minutes have passed, some may need to look at the number line to realise this is almost the 20 minutes up). If students have to use a stopwatch to time something, be aware that some might not know when to expect the number to show up (e.g. some might not know the numbers 26, 27, 28 mean they are getting close to the 30 seconds they have to time. Encourage students to refer to the number line to help them).

- Explain the measuring equipment you are using. Some rulers, weighing scales and other equipment do not label every number. Weighing scales, for example, may only label every 50 grams. Some students may not be able to work out how to measure 240 grams of something. Explain what number the smaller lines on your scales go up in and draw this on the board to demonstrate before expecting students to use these accurately.

- Reinforce and revisit how to read charts, tables and graphs whenever possible.

- Provide concrete mathematical equipment. This is not just a must in maths lessons. Equipment such as cubes, number squares, plastic money, counting beads, calculators and times table squares can all be useful across the curriculum. Have this equipment accessible and available to students across subjects and encourage students to use these as and when they need to.

GROUP WORK

Working with others is an important aspect of school life. Students are often asked to work in groups to complete tasks in class. Working as a group means larger projects can be completed, and is often essential in subjects such as music (playing in an orchestra), drama (taking part in plays) and PE (team sports). At other times students may be asked to work with others in order to share ideas, extend their thinking and support the learning process. In addition, the ability to work with others is a useful skill in itself and provides an opportunity to work on communication, co-operation and negotiation skills.

Naturally, for students who think, learn and relate to others differently than the majority, group work can sometimes be a difficult aspect of school life which can cause distress and frustration. Here are some of the difficulties students can experience:

- Understanding the language used by others.

- Understanding 'hidden meanings' such as jokes, sarcasm and inference.

- Expressing themselves through spoken language.

- Feeling misunderstood by others in the group.

- Keeping up with the dynamics of group conversation – conversation can flow too quickly for some to process and participate.

- Understanding and using conversational skills such as turn-taking, seeking clarification, body language, facial expression, politeness and appropriate levels of formality.

- Lacking assertiveness to express their thoughts and opinions.

- Wanting to focus on the task in hand and not enjoying the social aspect of group work.

- Feeling they could complete the task quicker alone.

- Becoming frustrated with others who are not concentrating on the task.

- Finding it difficult to concentrate on the task and so frustrating others in the group.

- Being unable to compromise and negotiate on how the task should be done.

- Worrying that others will not do their share of the work and will bring their grades down.

- Experiencing sensory overload from working with others (e.g. too much noise and interaction, and being unable to filter out background noise).

- Finding it difficult to multitask and to talk while doing activities.

- Feeling uncomfortable around others.

- Worrying what others may think of them.

- Not wanting to show that they have not understood the task or have difficulty with an aspect of the work.

Team sports in PE lessons can bring some challenges of their own. As well as some of the difficulties listed above, some neurodivergent students can also experience some of the following:

- Difficulties with motor skills such as finding it difficult to throw, catch or hit a ball.

- Having an unusual gait when walking or running.

- Poor balance.

- Difficulties with knowing where their body is in space and in relation to others – they might stand too close or too far away from others, they might find it difficult to know where to place themselves in relation to others and equipment.

- Being uncomfortable with physical touch.

- Not understanding the rules, or understanding the rules and feeling that others are not keeping to these.

- Sensory difficulties meaning that PE kits, specialist clothing or equipment is uncomfortable and prevents them from relaxing.

- Finding that team games happen too quickly for them to keep up.

- Feeling they have let their team members down.

- Being upset with team members who made mistakes.

- Being slow to get changed and dressed.

- Being picked last for teams or feeling other students do not want them on their team.

These are all real difficulties for many students and can put some off taking part in group work and team games altogether. This section contains some general principles to take into account when planning group work.

Allocate the groups

A student's self-esteem is likely to take a knock if they are constantly picked last for teams or if other students get into groups and leave them out. When this happens, it is easy to feel that nobody wants to work with you and that you are unpopular. Combat this by having the adults allocate the groups and teams. This has the added benefit of adults being able to manipulate teams and groups so that there is an even spread of abilities and experiences in each one, or that students of similar abilities work together, depending on the task in hand.

Use supportive peers

Although being able to work with a wide range of people is a useful skill, this needs to be built up slowly and not all students will be ready to work with anybody. Some staff can argue that students need to learn to work with everybody 'because that's how it is in real life – you can't pick and choose'. However, not all students are able to do this and insisting on it can cause increased distress. If students have to work with students whom they feel uncomfortable with, then the increased anxiety they experience is likely to outweigh any possible benefits of 'learning to work with anybody'. Create groups in which students are working with supportive peers. This way, students can improve their group working skills in a safer, more comfortable environment, building up their skills and confidence to work with others.

Teach the expectations of group work to all

Students are often asked to work in groups, perhaps without being taught or reminded about what this actually means. Before expecting students to work in groups, teach the whole class about what this means. Have a discussion about rules for working in groups. Try creating role plays of poor group work and effective group work. What was happening in the first? What was better in the second?

Revisit and reinforce these group work expectations before each group working task to remind all students.

Create a group agreement

Some classes may benefit from creating a 'group work agreement' to formalise their expectations. Ask students what they think is important when working with others. This may include:

- giving everybody a turn to speak

- not interrupting when somebody else is talking

- listening carefully to everybody's ideas

- everybody doing a fair share of the work

- asking questions when you do not understand

- respecting everybody's opinion

- disagreeing politely

- helping other team members to join in

- taking responsibility for a job

- telling others when there is a problem

- acting on constructive feedback

- helping others

- solving problems together.

These 'rules' will probably differ depending on the age of students and the subject area. Revisit these expectations before and during group work. Display them visibly on the wall or on tables. Praise students explicitly when you catch them following these expectations. Remember that improving the group work skills of all students, will help those who have difficulties, as they will be surrounded by others who are acting as positive role models.

Encourage reflection

As well as reinforcing group work rules before the task, build in times after the task when you encourage students to reflect on their group working skills. This can be done as a whole class discussion, within the smaller groups or on an individual basis. Ask students to identify what they think they are improving at or what went well. Is there anything that they are going to try differently next time to improve their group work?

Start small and build up slowly

Working in a group requires many skills, and the communication and interaction demands of this can be too much for some students some of the time. Allow students to build up their skills slowly. Some might begin by working with a supportive partner, before joining with another pair or with a third person. Others may begin by completing individual tasks which are then put together to make a larger, group piece of work.

Give specific roles

Students may also benefit from being given a specific role within the group. This might be a specific task which is allocated to each group member, or a specific role. Roles might include those such as timekeeper (keeping track of time and telling the group how long is left), notetaker (noting down the key points of the discussion), discussion leader (who makes sure everybody takes a turn to speak) or others depending on the activity and age group of students. Make sure that students are clear about exactly what they need to do for each role. Having a specific role can make it easier for some to participate and it brings some more structure to the task.

Make sure all understand the task

One of the biggest misunderstandings during group work often stems from students misinterpreting the task. This can cause conflict and confusion within the group. Ensure that students know:

- exactly what the group task is

- how long they have to spend on the task

- what the expected outcome is (e.g. a concrete piece of work, notes made from a discussion, an agreement reached, a plan made, verbal feedback to the class)

- what is expected of each group member

- for larger tasks, how the work will be assessed.

Ask students to explain in their own words what the task is. Support students who have a weak understanding of time by displaying a visual timer. Written and visual instructions (such as using a task board) are also helpful.

Cultivate a positive atmosphere

Creating an overall calm, positive atmosphere in your classroom will have a positive impact on group work as well as everything else. Encourage all students to get into the habit of asking when they are unsure about something, promote helpfulness and friendliness, and reiterate that it is ok to make mistakes and that it is ok to have different opinions.

TOP TIP! Keep in mind the overall aim of the activity in hand when deciding whether or not to insist on group work. What do you want students to learn from the task and what is the most important thing you want them to get out of it? If, for example, the main aim of a set of PE lessons is for students to keep fit and develop an enthusiasm for sport, then insisting on team sports may in fact put some students off exercise for life. Include a mix of activities so that students who find that team games provoke anxiety can still experience the enjoyment of exercising. Some students work better independently and you might want to let them do this when possible so that you can assess their academic capabilities more accurately. Group work is an important skill but remember that this can be extremely difficult for some students and might need to be built up slowly.

INDEPENDENCE AND ORGANISATION

Some neurodivergent students can experience differences in their executive functioning skills. These are the self-regulation skills needed for planning, preparing, organising and prioritising tasks.

Without appropriate executive functioning skills, students can find it difficult to work independently or to complete tasks. This can be extremely frustrating as they might feel they are never able to demonstrate what they know. Additional factors such as low self-esteem and a lack of confidence can also contribute to some students finding it difficult to work independently. Others may have become over-reliant on adult support and have not had the opportunity to develop self-regulation skills themselves.

There are many other students who will also benefit from being taught skills to support their personal organisation, so the suggestions which follow are all suitable to be used with the whole class. This section illustrates ways of supporting independent working skills in the mainstream classroom. Memory skills and homework are considered in separate sections.

Supporting independent work in the classroom
Visual timetables

Visual timetables are not just for young children but can benefit all ages when displayed in age-appropriate ways. A visual timetable is a timetable for the day (or week for older students) which often includes pictures or symbols as well as written words. It is not enough to simply display a visual timetable on the wall; it needs to be referred to throughout the day to have maximum effect. Discuss the timetable as you lay it out at the beginning of the day. This is a great opportunity to explain what is coming up and in what order. You can also tell students about any changes to routine or special events. Refer to where you are throughout the day by moving an arrow along or removing the cards for activities once you have done them. Display the timetable prominently at eye level for students so that they can refer to it too. This can help students who, for example, come in after break or lunch time having no idea what the next lesson is going to be. Older students may also benefit from visual timetables placed on their tables or in their planners. Encourage and remind students to refer to these throughout the day to get the right equipment out and, for older students, to get to the right classroom.

Task boards

A task board simply breaks down a task into smaller, more manageable chunks and can again be made appropriate for all age groups. For younger students a task board may comprise pictures or symbols, indicating which equipment they need (scissors, glue, crayons, pen, books, etc.) and what order to do tasks (cut out the picture, stick it in, write a caption, colour it in, etc.). These could be displayed on the board or a copy could be placed on each table or given to individuals. They can act as a visual reminder of the instructions, meaning that students can work more independently, not having to ask what to do next.

Older students can be taught how to create their own task boards. They might start by listing the equipment they need and then break down a task into smaller steps, making a numbered list. This can be done with adult support or as a whole class activity until students feel confident making their own. Having a task board written out in this way can make larger tasks seem more manageable and can help those who are unsure where to start and in which order to carry out tasks. Encourage students to tick off each stage once they have completed it so that they can see how far they are through a task.

'Have a go' attitude

Establishing a 'have a go' attitude in your classroom can also support independence. Praise students for having a go rather than waiting for adult support. Reiterate that it is ok to make mistakes and that this is an expected part of the learning process – some students are unwilling to have a go alone as they are worried about getting things wrong. Build an atmosphere in which students feel comfortable in asking for clarification when they do not understand.

Provide helpful resources

Many resources which have already been mentioned in this book can support students to work independently. These can include dictionaries, thesauruses, electronic spellcheckers, visual lists of usual vocabulary, screenreading technology and voice-text software. Make sure that it is a normal part of everyday classroom practice for students to use these resources and that they are available to all to remove any stigma. Remember to teach students how to use these resources effectively – students will avoid any resources or technology which they feel slow them down or aren't helpful, so will need to practise using these.

Support the planning stage

Providing additional support at the planning stage of tasks can help students to work more independently when it comes to the task itself. Here are some ideas:

- Ensure that the task has been understood by all students.

- Show what to do rather than just telling.

- Show completed examples of the task so that students know what they are aiming for.

- Discuss each step on the task board, encouraging students to ask any questions they might have.

- Generate ideas and possibilities, collecting these on the board or on an ideas sheet.

- Create opportunities for students to talk through their ideas with peers or adults.

- Create a mindmap of ideas or useful vocabulary.

- Have a planning template for students to record their ideas.

- Use a storyboard before writing a story for students to draw small pictures or write key words for each event.

- Use a writing frame for students to make brief notes or pictures of what they will include in each paragraph.

Remember to encourage students to refer to these planning aids as they complete the actual task. Some students spend a lot of time planning but do not necessarily transfer these ideas to the final piece.

Teach self-organisation strategies

Teach students how to organise themselves. Strategies may be as simple as ticking items off a list once they have done them, or using a Post-it® note as a visual reminder of a task they need to do later that day. Older students may learn strategies such as setting an alarm reminder on their phone to remind them to get their equipment ready each evening for school the next day.

Build in time for checking work

Get students into the mindset of realising a task is not complete until they have checked or proofread it. You might provide a checklist to enable students to check their work more independently. Depending on the task and age of students, it could include questions such as:

- Have you written a title?

- Have you started sentences with a capital letter?

- Have you checked any spellings you were unsure of in a dictionary?

- Have you asked a partner to read it aloud to check it makes sense?

TOP TIP! Make it easy for students to organise themselves. Those students who will really benefit from having a planner and timetable are those likely to lose them easily! Have spare copies available on display in the classroom. There can be a fine line between supporting students and reinforcing poor organisation. It might seem quicker and easier for adults to organise a student who is forgetful and loses equipment. Adults supporting the student may keep his books and equipment for him, not letting him take them out of the classroom. They might get his equipment out for him and liaise with parents about what needs to be brought in the next day. Although this may reduce anxiety for the student and means he avoids failure, if done in the long term he will find it hard to build up personal organisation skills of his own. Try to teach these skills slowly and encourage the student to find strategies that work for him as an individual.

MEMORY

There are different types of memory: long-term memory, procedural memor and episodic memory, for example. One type of memory which can affect many students and their learning is the idea of working memory (short-term memory). Difficulties with working memory can mean it takes longer to achieve automaticity in learning things such as times tables, a new language or rules of games. Working memory is also the type of memory that we need to 'hold' information in our heads, such as numbers when working out a maths problem.

So what can you do to support students in this area?

- Use visual support as some difficulties can mean that just words alone are harder to process.

- Provide clear written instructions for tasks. This could also be in the form of a visual task board. This sort of visual and written reminder can reduce the memory load on students. It means they can focus on carrying out one step at a time, rather than worrying about forgetting what to do next. It also helps students who would otherwise miss out stages of a task or would struggle to work independently.

- Give one instruction at a time and keep instructions clear.

- Teach note-making techniques. It can be difficult for students to remember what has been said, decide what is important and then write it down. Remind students that notes can be pictures, diagrams and single words. They do not have to worry about spelling.

- Encourage students to note down key numbers when doing maths, or key words, so that they are not trying to hold lots of pieces of information in their heads.

Other students can have difficulties retaining information from one lesson to the next. What can you do to support those students?

- Recap and link back to previous learning at the beginning of lessons.

- Summarise key points throughout the lesson.

- Highlight the key points in different ways.

- Teach in a multisensory way to provide as many 'hooks' for the information as possible. Show as well as tell.

- Link new information to a student's own experiences.

- Provide helpful resources such as photographs, pictures, diagrams and key word lists to support students' memory.

- Take photographs of students carrying out practical tasks, role plays or other activities and stick these in exercise books for students to annotate. A photograph can help students to remember what they did and what they learned.

- Provide checklists for students to refer to.

- Teach memory strategies such as visualisation, verbal rehearsal, counting on fingers or mnemonics to support students to remember key information. Creating mindmaps or highlighting key information can also be useful for students.

TEACHING AND LEARNING FOR NEURODIVERSITY CHECKLIST

Do you:

☐ Produce written materials (printed on paper and displayed onscreen) which are clear and easy to read?

☐ Give sufficient time for reading and writing tasks?

☐ Read aloud instructions and information?

☐ Encourage students to ask about new words and to use dictionaries and spellcheckers?

☐ Encourage use of screenreading technology and voice-text software for those who would benefit?

☐ Provide key word lists with visuals so that spelling is not a barrier?

☐ Create opportunities for talk and discussion before writing tasks?

☐ Use planning frames and writing frames to prepare for writing tasks?

☐ Use a range of teaching approaches and opportunities to learn in ways other than reading and writing?

☐ Provide number lines, number squares and timelines across the curriculum?

☐ Use visual timers to support students to understand how long they have on a task?

☐ Provide concrete mathematical equipment and resources?

☐ Teach group work skills explicitly?

☐ Allocate the groups and ensure students are working with supportive peers?

☐ Allocate specific roles for group work and ensure all are clear on the expectations?

☐ Create a positive atmosphere in your classroom where students feel comfortable to ask for help and to make mistakes?

☐ Use task boards and other written instructions to support independence and organisation?

☐ Refer to visual timetables throughout the day?

☐ Teach students how to use strategies to support memory?

KEY POINTS

- Reading, writing and maths skills are essential across the curriculum. Every subject requires these skills at some time or another. Many students can have difficulty with different aspects of reading, writing or maths. There are many strategies and resources which can be used in the classroom to support students in these areas, whatever subject you are teaching.

- Working in a group or team is an important skill but can be extremely difficult for some students who have difficulty communicating, expressing themselves, interpreting others and keeping up with the dynamics of group conversation. Students can also experience low self-esteem and friendship difficulties, meaning that they feel even more uncomfortable working with others. In PE, some students find that motor and spatial difficulties add to their discomfort in team sports. Build up group work skills slowly and be aware that it is not every student's preferred method of learning.

- Some students can have difficulty with personal organisation and working independently. There are many strategies and resources you can use in the mainstream classroom to teach and improve executive functioning skills.

6

STUDENT WELLBEING

In this chapter you will learn:

- why wellbeing can be harder to achieve for neurodivergent students than for others

- how to promote positive attitudes towards neurodiversity

- how to improve wellbeing in a neurodiverse student population

- how to empower students so that they feel happy and comfortable about their individuality.

WHAT IS WELLBEING?

Wellbeing is often talked about and can mean many different things. In this chapter we take wellbeing to mean that students feel safe, supported, happy and confident. Having a good sense of wellbeing does not mean feeling 'happy' all of the time but includes experiencing the whole range of human emotions and being able to cope with and manage these effectively and in line with your age and development.

Evidence suggests that neurodivergent students can feel less happy and have lower self-esteem than their more neurotypical counterparts. One study even suggests that children and young people with special educational needs can be up to six times more likely than their peers to experience mental health difficulties (NASS 2015). Young people on the autism spectrum, for example, have been shown to be more likely than their peers to experience mental health difficulties such as depression, anxiety or obsessive compulsive disorder (Kim *et al.* 2000) and those who are dyslexic can be more likely to experience lower self-esteem and can find learning stressful (Reid 2013). Similar evidence exists for many other neurodivergent conditions and labels.

So what are some of the reasons for neurodivergent students experiencing low levels of wellbeing?

- Not being able to do things (e.g. reading, catching a ball, socialising, concentrating, etc.) that appear to come so easily to their peers, no matter how hard they try.

- Finding it difficult to make and maintain friendships.

- Lacking a supportive friendship group to discuss events and to make sense of situations and experiences.

- Being compared, directly and indirectly, to their peers.

- Feeling that they are not able to demonstrate their ability or potential despite trying hard.

- Misunderstanding situations and other people.

- Getting 'into trouble' for things that they do not understand.

- Feeling misunderstood.

- Finding it difficult to express themselves clearly.

- Feeling isolated and left out.

- Feeling different and not understanding why.

- Being told that they are 'different', 'odd' or that there is 'something wrong' with them.

- Learning in an education system and living in a society which do not value their strengths or ways of interpreting the world.

- Being more vulnerable to bullying.

- Perhaps having less independence than their peers and feeling less in control of their own lives.

- Finding change and new experiences more stressful to deal with

Without the right support, many neurodivergent students may experience low self-esteem, anxiety, worry or depression, meaning that they do not enjoy school or do not manage to reach their potential. At worst this can lead to school refusal, missing out on education and more serious and long-lasting mental health difficulties. However, it should not be assumed that all neurodivergent students will inevitably have lower mental wellbeing and self-esteem and there is plenty that can be done to support students. In this chapter we consider several different components: how schools can improve wellbeing in a neurodiverse student population, how we can empower students to feel in control of their present and future and how we can promote positive attitudes towards neurodiversity.

> **TOP TIP!** Don't forget the basics. Eating healthily, keeping active and getting enough good-quality sleep can all have a huge impact on our wellbeing. Not getting enough sleep, for example, affects not only tiredness levels but also mood, concentration and irritability. Teach students about the importance of sleep, encouraging them to switch off their mobile devices before going to bed. Create opportunities for students to try out and take part in a wide range of physical exercise – martial arts, dance, yoga, running, Zumba, tennis, football, hiking – individual students will have different preferences.

IMPROVING WELLBEING
Reducing anxiety in the classroom

Students' wellbeing levels can vary from lesson to lesson and can be affected by many different factors, some of which may be beyond our control but some of which we can eliminate or reduce. In the classroom learning environment there can be many anxieties for neurodiverse students, all of which can combine to increase feelings of frustration, worry or anxiety. Previous chapters have already considered what we can do to support students' understanding and learning. We now look at some further strategies which can be beneficial in reducing anxiety.

- **Use visual timetables.** Going through a visual timetable at the beginning of the day can support all students to know what they will be doing so that there are no unexpected surprises. This can also be an opportunity for them to ask questions about the day, feel prepared and alleviate any anxieties they might have. Ensure that older students also have personal and class timetables so that they can organise themselves.

- **Share the outline of the lesson.** Tell students what you will be doing in the lesson and in which order. Give time boundaries so that students understand roughly how long will be spent on each activity. This supports them to orient themselves in the lesson and realise that their less favourite activities will not go on forever! We all feel better if we know what is coming up and what we are going to be expected to do.

- **Use task boards and other visual instructions.** Having a written and visual reminder of instructions can reduce the anxiety of forgetting what has to be done.

- **Have clear and consistent routines.** Having clear routines and a structured day can support many students. Get you classes into good habits, so that they know what to do when entering the classroom and before leaving, for example. Ensure that expectations and routines are consistent across all staff and classes to avoid confusion.

- **Prepare students for new situations.** We can all feel anxious about new situations (just think back to the last time you began a new job or had to travel somewhere new). Support students by explaining to them any new events or situations that are coming up. Remember that some students will benefit not only from opportunities to ask questions but also opportunities to rehearse and practise for new situations. Books and videos can often be effective in supporting students to know what to expect, as can taking part in role plays and drama activities. Particular situations which could cause anxiety are often the transition to a new school or class, school trips or days on which the usual timetables are suspended.

- **Explain rules and expectations.** It benefits all students if rules and expectations are clearly explained. Tell students exactly why certain rules are in place and the benefits of these. Some students may find it difficult to understand why they need to follow certain rules, so open up a dialogue rather than simply insisting on acquiescence. It is also important to ensure that rules, rewards and sanctions are all applied consistently and fairly, as many students will have difficulty understanding why rules are different in different situations or for different people. Remember, too, that if a rule doesn't make sense or isn't regularly applied it may be time to replace the 'rule' or expectation with something that is applied more consistently.

- **Support understanding of the unwritten rules.** Many students can have difficulty in picking up on those 'unwritten rules' of school life, such as not telling the teacher who it was who aimed the paper aeroplane at the back of their head! This sort of thing can cause fallings out and misunderstandings amongst pupils; some students might need to have it explained explicitly why their peers were upset with them!

- **Use Social Stories™ and Comic Strip Conversations.** These methods, first devised by Carol Gray, were originally intended to support students on the autism spectrum but can help a wide range of young people to understand upcoming situations and to unpick events that have happened. They can be adapted for different age groups and abilities.

- **Cultivate an 'it's ok to ask for help' atmosphere.**
  If students feel they are going to be blamed, judged or criticised for asking for help, then they are likely to continue to struggle on, increasing their anxiety and frustration. Create opportunities for students to ask for help from adults and peers, both during whole class work and independent work.

TOP TIP! Remember that some students can be particularly sensitive to sensory input and too much of this can increase anxiety and frustration. Keep background noise to a minimum, turn off fluorescent lighting and create quiet spaces for students to work and socialise in.

Social times

Social times, such as break and lunch times, can often be the times of the day when neurodivergent students feel most anxious, different or vulnerable. These are often less structured times and the playground has a whole set of different rules and expectations from the classroom. It might be the time when students notice any social differences more acutely or when bullying occurs. The physical environment of the playground can also be overwhelming for some.

These strategies can support students during social times:

- Create quiet spaces for students to use if they prefer to spend social times alone or engaged in a quiet activity such as reading. Remember to accept this as just as valid a preference as socialising and ensure these areas are open to everybody to reduce any stigma. Make sure too that quiet areas remain quiet.

- Having a range of more structured activities on offer can also be beneficial. These could include arts and crafts clubs, homework club, computer club, sports clubs or organised outdoor games.

- Try having 'break time buddies' or a 'buddy bench'. Children can sit on the bench to let others know that they would like to join in with games or chat to other people. Encourage other pupils to monitor the bench and support any child who is sitting on the bench to join in.

Promoting happiness, resilience and a growth mindset

Happiness and positive attitudes

We often use the word 'happiness' and say that we want our young people to be 'happy' without thinking too much about what we actually mean by happiness. It can be a difficult concept to define and happiness means many different things to different people. One person, for example, may say that they are happy when they are in a crowded football stadium watching their favourite team. Another person might find the same situation extremely boring!

Greek philosopher Aristotle identified that there are different sorts of happiness – short-term happiness (having fun, experiencing pleasure, doing enjoyable activities) and longer-term happiness (overall living a good, purposeful and meaningful life). Modern positive psychologists also recognise that being 'happy' is not only about short-term pleasurable pursuits but also about 'flourishing' as a person (Seligman 2002).

For the purposes of this section, we interpret 'happiness' in both senses – feeling 'happy' doing particular activities and that more general feeling of being safe, supported, comfortable and generally feeling happy in our own skin. Being 'happy' is not about eliminating more 'negative' feelings and emotions altogether, as that is both unrealistic and counterproductive. Rather, people who are 'happy' experience the full range of human emotions but are able to cope appropriately with these and regain a sense of equilibrium.

Perhaps most important when considering the topic of happiness is that a neurotypical view of happiness is not imposed on neurodivergent students. It is essential to recognise and accept that different things make different people happy and that these are all equally valid. Take, for example, a student on the autism spectrum. This student may feel no natural connection with other people and may enjoy spending significant amounts of time in their own company. More 'neurotypical' values might consider having a large friendship group and spending time with others is what makes a person happy and that spending time alone must indicate that they are unhappy. In this case, it may be that the opposite is actually true – that spending a lot of time around others may in fact increase this student's anxiety levels. One of the most important things we can do as professionals, therefore, is to accept and embrace the fact that every student interprets the world, other people, feelings and emotions differently – and that all of these ways are equally valid.

So what can we do to support students in increasing their happiness levels?

- Support students to identify and recognise their strengths! Some neurodivergent students may have low self-esteem or focus on their weaknesses (such as finding reading, learning or socialising difficult) rather than their strengths. Other students may have strengths which have never been perceived as such (such as a student being told they are pedantic or argumentative, instead of realising that they have good attention to detail and are able to identify inconsistencies – a vital skill for many careers). Help students to identify their strengths – positive characteristics which are transferable into many aspects of life. Some examples of strengths can include: creativity, adaptability, love of learning, teamwork, reliability, justice, kindness, spirituality, gratitude, critical thinking, open mindedness, perseverance, humour and honesty. More detailed lists can be found in books and online.

- Help students to identify what makes them happy and to build in more of these activities into their week. Perhaps there are activities they used to do but do not have access to any longer or perhaps there are opportunities to try out new activities which could become hobbies and interests.

- Reinforce what is going well. We all tend to have an inbuilt negativity bias that means we often remember the one negative rather than the ten positive things which have happened! Encourage students to identify what is going well and what they are grateful for, to support more balanced thinking. This could be done as an activity at the end of the day or at the end of a lesson – students identify three things that went well. Help students to recognise the part they played so that they begin to see the influence they can have on what happens to them (e.g. try to move from 'People played with me at lunch time' to 'I had the confidence to ask to join in a game at lunch time'; or instead of 'I got 6 out of 10 on my spellings', encourage 'I spent 20 minutes practising my spellings last night and got more right than last week').

- Promote an 'it's normal to be different' atmosphere within your classroom and setting. Accept all different preferences and encourage this thinking in all of your students. A simple statement such as, 'Yes, some people like to play football at lunch time, others like to chat to friends, other like to read, others like to be by themselves. We are all different and like different things', can go a long way in helping students to feel that their preferences are as normal and as valid as anybody else's.

- Try not to reinforce stereotypes. Don't assume that individuals will have certain strengths or weaknesses just because of the label they have been given. For example, do not assume that all dyslexic students will be creative and good at art, or that all students with ADHD will enjoy PE lessons. Equally, do not assume that all autistic students have no friends or that all dyslexic students dislike reading! Labels and diagnoses often reinforce prejudices and stereotypes which can be unhelpful for the individuals in question.

- Avoid mislabelling feelings. It can be easy to assume that everybody must be experiencing feelings in the same way that we do. Take, for example, a student who was due to go to a party. The party is cancelled and the adult says to the student, 'Oh, what a shame, you must be feeling so disappointed.' This may be true of some students but this student may, in fact, be feeling relieved. Perhaps they were dreading going to the party as they find the environment and crowds of people anxiety inducing. This student may begin to distrust their own feelings, assuming that they are 'wrong' as they have been told they should be experiencing a different feeling.

- Create opportunities for students to express themselves creatively. Activities such as crafting, sewing, playing and listening to music, drama, art and dance have all been shown to improve feelings of happiness and wellbeing, as has spending time outdoors in nature. Encourage students to try out these activities, or set up more opportunities for them to access these types of activities, such as an after-school gardening club. Reading has also been shown to increase wellbeing as we encounter characters who are experiencing similar thoughts and feelings to our own, realising we are not the only ones to think in a certain way (Kidd and Castano 2013). Journalling, too, has been shown to have wellbeing benefits as this can help us to make sense of our thoughts and feelings (Roberts 2015). These may be activities to suggest to some of your students.

• Ensure students know where and how to access support. There may be various support services available in your setting – counsellors, psychologists, therapists, school nurses, career counsellors, and academic support such as homework clubs. Make sure that students are aware of what is available and how to access these. Having open access or a drop-in facility can make these services more accessible to students.

Resilience and a growth mindset

We can also support our students to develop resilience and a growth mindset. Resilience is the ability to 'bounce back' and to regain a sense of balance after difficult events and experiences. In a growth mindset (Dweck 2006) we believe that our thoughts, skills, qualities and abilities can be improved and cultivated through effort and that we can change and grow through experiences.

Thoughts typical of individuals in a fixed mindset might include:

'I'm rubbish at maths.'

'I can't do languages.'

'I'll never get any better at this so there's no point me trying.'

'I'm good at this so I don't have to practise.'

On the other hand, thought typical of individuals in a growth mindset may include:

'I can get better at this.'

'I'm still learning how to speak French.'

'I can't do this yet but I can keep trying.'

'I can learn from mistakes I make.'

So how can we support students to develop more resilient thinking and a growth mindset?

- Cultivate an 'it's great to make mistakes' atmosphere in your classroom. Reinforce to students that it is only through having a go, trying out different possibilities and getting things wrong that we learn. This is not only true for academic learning but in other areas of our personal and social lives too. Focus on the process of learning rather than the product. Remind students how many great inventions and ideas came about from individuals making what they first perceived as 'mistakes'.

- Show students how to learn from both success and failure. When things go well, reflect on what the student did to create that outcome. What can they be doing more of? When things do not go so well, reflect on that too. What could the student try differently next time?

- Support students to identify all of their achievements, no matter how small. Keep a journal, diary, scrapbook, yearbook or class chart. Remember that achievements are not just the final outcome of a task but the effort and skills that went into it. Achievements are also not just limited to those in academic spheres. Recording these helps students to recognise what they are doing well (e.g. 'I walked to school by myself', 'I worked independently on writing in English for 15 minutes', 'I asked for help when I was stuck', 'I helped to show the new student what to do in class').

- Support independence and problem-solving skills. Support students, while at the same time equipping them with skills to use more independently over time. Help students to generate their own solutions and options and to create their own action plans, breaking down larger tasks or problems into smaller steps to work on.

- Model a growth mindset in your own language. Young people will pick up on how adults around them talk and think. If you are saying things like 'I'm no good at maths' or

'I've never been able to do division', then you cannot expect them to change their thinking.

- Use 'yet' or 'still' rather than 'can't' and 'don't'. Students may interpret statements such as, 'You can't do languages' or 'She doesn't get maths' quite literally and assume these are fixed states which will always stay the same. Instead, use statements such as, 'You are still learning how to speak Spanish' or 'She isn't secure on multiplication yet.'

EMPOWERING STUDENTS

Taking on board students' views and opinions can be one of the most important things we do, both at an individual and collective level. On an individual level this means ensuring that students feel they are listened to and have somebody to talk to if they feel they need it. They feel their views are taken seriously and that they receive the support that they need. This again is something which should be offered to all students, and not only those with identified needs. On a collective level, students feel involved in decision making, on a group, class and whole school level. Some neurodivergent students may not necessarily feel that their views are represented on student councils or other committees.

TOP TIP! Ensure that your setting does not take a tokenistic approach to student voices. Students should be taught to become active participants in their school setting, learning how to reflect, interpret and make thoughtful and informed decisions. Try to ensure that student voice schemes do not simply collect information without acting on it. Students who spend time taking part in the decision-making process will have an expectation that they are going to be listened to and that something is going to change. If nothing does, they are likely to be disappointed and lose trust in the adults around them.

Listening to students

Active listening

How adults listen to students can make a big difference to whether or not they perceive they are being taken seriously and that their views are valued and accepted. Sometimes it can be difficult truly to 'listen' to students, perhaps because of time constraints, distractions or simply not feeling we have the skills or knowledge to support them. The technique of 'active listening', often used in counselling and psychotherapy, can easily be transferred to everyday situations and can improve our listening skills:

- Try to ignore distractions. Distractions may be external (other people, the phone ringing, things in your environment) or internal (thoughts about other things, what you will eat for dinner, what else you have to do). If you notice your thoughts wandering, bring your attention back to the person you are listening to.

- Check your non-verbal communication. Look at your body language. Do you look interested? Are you trying to do something else at the same time or regularly looking at your phone or the clock? Are you looking in their direction? Some students can find too much eye contact uncomfortable, so try to achieve a balance.

- Be honest. If you lose concentration or cannot follow what a student is saying, ask them to tell you again.

- Avoid leading questions. Closed questions (which require a yes/no) answer may not encourage students to go any further. Leading questions may encourage a student to say or think in a certain way (e.g. 'Maths is always really boring, isn't it?', 'You like to have friends, don't you?'). Use open questions instead or simply ask students if there is anything more they would like to tell you.

- Avoid criticism or judgement. It can be easy to impose our own views and values on those we are listening to without realising we are doing so. Try to avoid anything that could sound critical or judgemental (e.g. 'Why did you think you could do that?', 'I think you should have…'). Listen instead and simply repeat or paraphrase what the student has said to show that you were listening.

- Don't try to offer solutions and advice. Active listening is about allowing the talker to express themselves and feel listened to. Don't feel that you have to jump in, offering solutions.

Listening to students can require time and, in some cases, specialist skills and knowledge outside your area of expertise. If you do not have the time to listen to a student, be honest with them and ensure they understand that you do value the fact that they would like to discuss something with you. You might like to suggest a more convenient time for them to come back (and make sure you stick to it!) or you might explain that there are certain people in the school (a counsellor or mentor, etc.) who have specialist skills and who may be able to offer more time and expertise. Support the student to access these people and check with the student at a later date whether they have been able to get support.

Student voice questionnaire

You could try using the survey below to collect students' views about their setting or adapt it for your particular students or environment. Remember that some students may benefit from having the questions read aloud (by a person or screenreader). If students need support in completing the survey and it cannot be adapted further, ensure that they are supported to complete it by a 'neutral' person, not by somebody whom they might want to please or anybody who might influence their answers.

★ *Student voice survey*

Name: Date:	Strongly disagree ☹	Disagree ☹	Agree ☺	Strongly agree ☺
I feel safe on my journey into school				
I feel safe walking around the corridors				
I feel comfortable/happy at break and lunch times				
There are enough quiet places to go when I need them				
I am told about what is happening in school and any changes to the school day				
I can easily find my way around school				
There are plenty of things to do at break and lunch times				
I can understand what I have to do in class. The instructions are clear				
I am able to use things in class that help me with my learning				
I am given enough time to do my work in class				
I feel confident to ask adults for help in class				
The classrooms are comfortable (not too bright/dark, not too hot/ cold, not too noisy, not too crowded)				
I know who I can speak to in school if I have a problem				

I know what I need to bring to school each day				
I have enough help with doing the homework that I get				
I understand why we have the rules we do and what is expected in school				
I am able to show my teachers what I have understood and learned				
I enjoy being in lessons				

What do you like about this school?

What do you dislike about this school?

Thinking about your answers to this survey, do you have any suggestions about how things could be improved?

Student self-audit

Use this survey to support students in identifying their own strengths, needs and what they would like more support with. Having filled in this survey, students could benefit from discussing their answers with a member of staff. How could their strengths be built on? What could help them with the areas they find difficult? The answers to these surveys could also indicate to staff what else the school can be doing to support students. Again, you might need to adapt this survey for some of your students.

★ *Student self-audit*

Name: Date:	I always find this difficult	Sometimes I can find this difficult	Mostly I am able to do this	I can always do this
Understanding the instructions teachers give				
Knowing what I have to do in class				
Asking for help in class				
Reading in class				
Writing in class				
Giving answers in class				
Working with a partner				
Working in a small group				
Giving a presentation in front of the class				
Finding and using the resources I need to help me with my learning in class				
Planning my work				
Taking part in discussion and debates				
Presenting my work neatly				
Working independently in class				
Finding information from the internet				
Presenting my work using a computer				

Revising for tests and exams				
Showing what I know in tests and exams				
Understanding what I have to do for homework				
Getting my homework handed in on time				
Bringing the right equipment to school				
Knowing what is happening in the school day				
Finding things I would like to do at break and lunch times				
Concentrating in class				
Making and keeping friends				
Talking to other students				
Getting involved in after-school clubs				
Getting the work finished in time				
Understanding the school rules				
What else are you good at in school?				
What else would you like more help with in school?				

All about me

Once students have considered their strengths and needs, they might like to create an 'all about me' profile which can be shared with adults who are working with them. This could be a suitable activity when beginning in a new year group, or to complete before the transition to a new class, year, key stage or school. Try to encourage students not simply to list subjects that they enjoy or find difficult, but to think about specific skills which go across subjects and situations (e.g. 'discussing the work with other students', 'using voice-text software', 'adults checking I have understood the instructions', 'being left to work by myself once I know what I am doing').

★ *All about me*

Name:	Class:
Things that I like:	Things that I enjoy in school:
Things that I find easy in school:	Things that help me to learn in class:
Things that I find difficult in school:	I would like to be helped in school by:
Other things I would like school staff to know about me are:	

TOP TIP! Remember that adult stress and wellbeing levels can have an impact on students. Adults (both parents and teachers) who are stressed, anxious or overworked are likely to find it more difficult to support students effectively. Ensure that you support staff wellbeing too.

CHECKLIST FOR PROMOTING STUDENT WELLBEING

Do you:

☐ Have clear and consistent routines in place across classrooms and year groups?

☐ Share information with students about changes to routine and new events?

☐ Share the outline of the lesson with students?

☐ Cultivate an 'it's ok to ask for help' atmosphere?

☐ Have a range of ways for students to ask for help (e.g. a worry box, mentors, support via email)?

☐ Ensure your classrooms are not overwhelming with sensory input?

☐ Have a range of activities on offer for break and lunch times?

☐ Ensure that all students know how to access the student counsellor, school nurse, learning mentors or other staff who can support various needs?

☐ Support staff to communicate in an open, honest way and listen to students appropriately?

☐ Provide support for staff who want to find out more about neurodiversity or who lack confidence in working with a diverse range of students?

☐ Promote teaching of resilience and a growth mindset?

☐ Collect student opinions about the school and act on these views?

☐ Ensure that a range of students are represented on student councils or other decision-making boards?

☐ Encourage students to reflect on their own strengths and needs?

☐ Promote independence and teach problem-solving skills?

☐ Create opportunities for students to share with staff their learning preferences and views?

☐ Ensure that positive attitudes towards neurodiversity and difference are promoted?

PROMOTING POSITIVE ATTITUDES TOWARDS NEURODIVERSITY

Throughout this book, we have considered new ways of approaching individual needs in schools. Rather than seeing conditions such as autism, dyslexia or ADHD as being disorders or disabilities, we consider these to be part of the natural diversity of the human population. Instead of being labelled and marginalised, this individuality should be recognised, accepted and valued. Numerous strategies have been suggested in this book about specific areas, but most important is the overall atmosphere of acceptance and diversity which permeates your setting. The overall ethos of a setting will support all students to feel supported and valued. The final chapter of this book, 'Whole School Approaches', explores what can be done on a whole school level to promote positive attitudes towards neurodiversity.

KEY POINTS

- Some students might experience anxiety in the classroom for a number of reasons. Many small changes to the physical environment, adult communication, routines and resources can all support to reduce anxiety levels.

- Neurodivergent students may have more difficulty than their peers in achieving positive attitudes, resilience and a growth mindset. There are many helpful ways in which adults can communicate which can promote these areas, as well as specific activities which can be beneficial.

- Happiness can mean different things to different people. It is important not to try to impose a neurotypical view of happiness onto neurodivergent students.

- Support students to recognise their strengths. Neurodivergent students might have a tendency to focus on their perceived weaknesses instead.

- Listening to students on different levels can be incredibly valuable to find out about individual needs and to support students better in general.

- Ensure that neurodivergent students are part of the decision-making process in your setting, but be careful that their participation is not just tokenism.

7

WORKING WITH HOME

In this chapter you will learn:

- about difficulties a neurodivergent student population can experience with homework and how to support students

- how to communicate with parents and carers of neurodivergent students, who might be neurodivergent themselves.

Neurodiversity does not end at the classroom door. Students who have different ways of thinking, learning and relating to others will experience these differences across all contexts and situations. Neurodiversity also does not disappear when students turn 18 and leave school. Our population as a whole is neurodiverse, with many adults also having 'neurodivergent' ways of processing, such as dyslexia, dyspraxia, ADHD or autism spectrum conditions. These are all lifelong ways of being. It is probable that many students have parents, carers or other family members who would consider themselves to be 'neurodivergent'. When communicating with home, education professionals need to be aware that some parents and carers may have similar differences to their children. Some may be in an ideal position to support their children, having had to develop their own coping strategies. Others may have had negative experiences of school which can affect their current attitude. In this chapter we look at how to communicate effectively with home and how to support a neurodiverse student body with homework and other tasks outside the classroom.

HOMEWORK

Difficulties neurodivergent students may experience with homework tasks include:

- not doing the task in time

- not having the correct equipment or resources at home

- forgetting to do it

- forgetting the instructions

- not understanding the instructions

- not knowing where to start

- worrying they might do it wrong

- not setting aside enough time to do the task

- lack of focus and being easily distracted.

These difficulties can affect all students at times, not only those who would be considered to be neurodivergent. In addition difficulties facing students may also include a lack of support at home, lack of a quiet place to concentrate, having no time due to other commitments, or simply not feeling that homework is useful, interesting or important! The ideas below are targeted at some of the specific difficulties neurodivergent students can experience but, again, will be useful for a large proportion of the student population.

Supporting homework

Allow sufficient time to explain the task

It often happens that we set homework tasks in the last few minutes of a lesson as students are packing up and getting ready to leave. This can mean that their attention is not on what we are saying and they are more concerned with thinking about what they are going to have for lunch or do after school. We might also find that our instructions are rushed and lack detail, perhaps not explaining things as well as we would usually do. Set aside sufficient time to explain and give out homework tasks within your lesson plan. Make sure that students see the relevance of homework tasks and that they are not just being set for the sake of setting homework. Link the task to what students have been or will be learning in class.

Check understanding

Remember that some students need extra processing time to make sense of instructions and information. Allow some reflection time after setting homework, giving students the opportunity to think about the task, make sense of it and ask any questions that occur to them. Check that students have understood by asking them to explain the task in their own words, perhaps to a partner to share understanding. Check in on students between setting the task and the final deadline, reminding them of the task set and asking if any questions have arisen from their work on it so far.

Show examples

We all do better when we have an example to work from. Think about when you are cooking or doing DIY. Which is easiest – to follow a process that is just written or one that has accompanying photographs? If you can visualise what you are aiming for, it can be easier to check that you are on the right track. When possible, show students examples of finished projects so that they can see what outcome they are aiming for.

Provide clear written instructions

Many students will have difficulty remembering verbal instructions or in making notes while a teacher is speaking. Providing clear written instructions for homework tasks means that students are guaranteed to have the correct instructions and information when they come to do the task. Look at Chapter 3 about producing clear written communication for neurodiversity. Use age-appropriate vocabulary. Keep sentences simple. Break down tasks into smaller steps. Ensure any visuals are helpful and relevant. Include a clear deadline and be specific about how much work you expect or how long students need to spend on the task.

Send home useful resources

Students will benefit from having helpful resources available, so send home what they might need for the task. It may be that they need word lists, their class exercise books or pages copied from a textbook. Without these some students will not be able to remember and recall all of the information from class, meaning their homework may demonstrate only memory skills rather than their understanding. Encourage students to use the resources at home that they do in class. Screenreaders and voice-text software are now inbuilt in most devices so should be available on home devices as well as in school. Lend out dictionaries and thesauruses if these aren't available at home.

Avoid time wasting

Some students can spend a lot of time working on a task without getting anywhere! This is often the case with internet-related research tasks when students have to find out about a topic. Students might find that they spend a lot of time looking for relevant websites, only finding ones which are too difficult to understand or which contain inaccurate information. This can then lead to time being wasted on having to sift through the mass of information out there. If using websites for research, find some child-friendly ones and provide the web addresses. This means students can concentrate on learning rather than internet surfing.

Use task boards

Task boards (discussed in more detail in the 'Independence and Organisation' section in Chapter 5) can be useful for homework tasks. A task board includes a list of required equipment followed by a breakdown of each stage of the task. These can support students who are overwhelmed by larger, unmanageable tasks. Suggest an amount of time for students to spend on each stage of the task.

Share tasks with parents

Most parents want to be able to support their child with homework but can find it difficult if the child is unable to remember or explain accurately what the task was or if they have lost the instructions on the way home! Help parents by providing clear written instructions which you send home or email out. Some schools post the homework tasks for the entire year on the school's virtual learning environment, meaning that parents can access these whenever they need to. Be aware, however, that not every parent has reliable access to the internet and some may prefer a paper version.

Teach useful strategies

Students will benefit from being taught strategies to help them to organise themselves. For some students this may be as simple as setting an alarm on their phone each evening to help them to remember to start their homework. Teach students strategies explicitly, such as ticking off items once done and how to use a calendar to prioritise work they need to do each evening.

Allow access to school resources

And, finally, remember that some students will simply find it difficult to work at home, perhaps because of a lack of quiet or simply because there are too many distractions. Provide opportunities for students to use the school library, computer suite or other facilities to do their homework – perhaps at lunch times or after school. Again, open this opportunity to all students and remind them that the facilities are there to be used. You could even open up the facilities to parents and carers too, providing the space and resources for them to work with their child on homework after school.

COMMUNICATING WITH HOME

Communicating with parents and carers is an essential part of any school's work. Good communication channels between home and school mean that information is passed on both ways. Parents feel informed about what is happening at school and know how best to support their child's education, and school is aware of parental wishes and concerns. Parents have a wealth of knowledge and insight into their child's behaviour and life and can often give school a greater insight into how their child experiences the world.

Supporting parents and carers

Many strategies and resources which are used in the school environment can also be used successfully in the home environment. Visual timetables, for example, or visual task boards could be used at home to make it clear to students the tasks they need to do each morning or each evening before bed. A visual list of equipment might help them to pack their school bag more independently. Strategies and resources which are used in the classroom, can also help with homework tasks. Share successful strategies with parents during open evening, parent evenings or drop-in mornings.

Encourage parents to share successful strategies that they are using at home with you. Again, these might transfer easily to the school setting.

Gathering views from parents and carers

A template like the one on the next page might be helpful in gathering views from parents and carers.

★ *Parental questionnaire*

Child's name:	Year group:
What are your child's strengths and interests?	
What does your child enjoy about school?	
What does your child find difficult or dislike about school?	
Does your child have any difficulty completing homework?	
What motivates your child at home? What does your child respond well to?	
Does your child use any effective resources or strategies at home which could also be used in school?	

Communicating with parents and carers

Remember that adults are just as neurodiverse as young people! Amongst the parents and carers you encounter, many will consider themselves neurodivergent, perhaps having a diagnosis of dyslexia, autism or ADHD themselves. Neurodiversity is sometimes not as obvious in the adult population as many have developed coping strategies which enable them to participate in society. However, this does not mean that they no longer have these differences. As we discussed at the beginning of this book, the school system has generally been designed for just one way of neurocognitive functioning, leaving others at a disadvantage. The same is true for how schools work with parents and carers – some may feel at a disadvantage because the systems set up are designed for only one way of being. Remember that some parents and carers may:

- need additional time to process written information

- lack confidence with reading and writing

- have difficulty interpreting numerical data

- need additional time to process verbal information

- find social interaction overwhelming

- have individual sensory needs

- prefer to communicate in a certain way (e.g. via email, face to face)

- have had negative experiences of education and the school system

- lack confidence to help their child academically or socially

- have had first-hand knowledge of what it feels like to be 'different'

- have developed effective coping strategies themselves which they can share with their children.

Considering how your school communicates with parents and carers can improve communication.

- Consider the written communication that you send home. Many adults have similar difficulties to younger people when it comes to reading, processing and understanding. Use a clear font and space out information making it easier to read. Use plain English and keep your sentence structure clear. Use bullet points or a list and stick to the important points. Make sure any written information sent home is clear, unambiguous and not 'waffle'.

- The same is relevant for the information posted on school websites, often parents' first stop to find out information.

Consider the fonts, backgrounds and layout used. Keep language clear and make the site easy to navigate.

- Some adults may prefer information to be sent in an email or text message as they can then change to their preferred font or background colour or use a screenreader to listen to the text rather than read it. Others, however, can find it difficult to read with the glare of a screen, so provide a variety of ways to communicate with parents.

- Provide a variety of ways for parents to contact the school. Not all will feel confident writing notes or emails. Others may find it uncomfortable to talk on the phone or to communicate face to face.

- Follow up any face-to-face meetings with a brief written summary of the main points covered and actions agreed. This can support adults who have differences in the way they process information.

- Not all adults are comfortable communicating in large groups, so provide opportunities for questions on a one-to-one basis after large meetings.

- Explain any graphs or charts that you use to show students' progress. Not only do some adults experience difficulties with numbers but the education system changes quickly and this sort of information can be new and meaningless to many parents and carers.

COMMUNICATING WITH PARENTS CHECKLIST

Do you:

☐ Send home clear instructions about homework tasks?

☐ Allow students to take home helpful resources to support homework tasks?

☐ Give clear expectations for homework tasks and suggest the most suitable websites to use?

☐ Make it easy for parents and carers to contact the school and find out about the homework which is set?

☐ Share useful strategies and resources with home?

☐ Ask parents and carers to share useful strategies and resources with school?

☐ Send home clear and unambiguous written letters, emails and information?

☐ Have an easy-to-navigate school website?

☐ Provide a variety of ways for parents and carers to contact the school?

☐ Explain data clearly to parents and carers?

KEY POINTS

- Homework can be a source of frustration and confusion for many students. There are many simple strategies teachers can use which can make a big difference to students' ability to complete tasks independently.

- Parents may be experiencing their own frustration at home if they have children who think, learn and relate to others in a different way to themselves. Schools can support by passing on useful strategies and resources which are used in the school setting. Information should also be gathered from parents as they are in the best position to understand how their child experiences the world. Many strategies used at home can also be transferred to the school context.

- Remember too that the entire population is neurodiverse, not just young people. Many parents and carers also have different ways of thinking, learning and relating to others. It is important that schools recognise this and adapt how they communicate accordingly.

8

WHOLE SCHOOL APPROACHES

In this chapter you will learn:

- how to implement a whole school approach to neurodiversity

- how to support staff to teach and work with a neurodiverse student population

- how to ensure school policies reflect the neurodiverse student population.

As when implementing any new policy or attitude within a school, success will often depend on those leading the initiative and the importance it is given within the setting. The previous chapters have discussed what a neurodiverse-friendly school looks like in practice. We have explored how adults communicate, effective teaching and learning practices, the physical environment and how to promote student wellbeing. We now look at the groundwork some schools may have to do to ensure that these practices are supported by the general ethos of the school or college.

Let's recap some of the key points to take into consideration:

- Humans all differ in the way that they think, learn and relate to others. This diversity is a completely normal aspect of human variation and needs to be expected.

- Within any class, therefore, you will find a large proportion of students who think, learn and interpret the world 'differently'.

- In the past this diversity has not always been recognised or accepted. Individuals who think differently can be placed at a disadvantage by living within systems that have been designed only for one way of being.

- Individuals who think differently have often been given labels (e.g. 'autism', 'dyslexia' or 'ADHD').

- These labels are not necessarily always helpful. There can be a huge range of diversity within these categories and labels can bring prejudices and stereotypes. In addition some individuals can have more than one label or might not meet the criteria for a certain label. Support should be given according to a student's needs, not their label.

- The neurodiversity paradigm encourages us to recognise individual differences as part of the natural diversity of the human population. These differences should be accepted, expected and anticipated.

- This shift in perspective means that schools and colleges need to anticipate this diversity and adjust their policies, practices and environments accordingly.

- Getting it right from the beginning will benefit a large number of students, reducing anxiety and improving academic, social and emotional development.

GETTING STAFF ON BOARD

You might be lucky to have an enthusiastic staff team who embrace the concept of neurodiversity and who welcome the opportunity to make changes to their everyday practice to make their teaching and learning more inclusive. Some, however, may be resistant to doing things differently. Here are some common attitudes which occur and how to combat them:

Responding to unhelpful attitudes

Unhelpful attitude	Possible strategies
'I don't teach students with special educational needs. They're the responsibility of the SENCO/ teaching assistants.'	• Remind staff that this is not true. The national teaching standards and SEN Code of Practice clearly state that all teachers are teachers of special educational needs (SEN) and retain responsibility for the progress of pupils in their class, even when they are supported by additional adults or are on the SEN register. • Some staff might not be aware of the range of needs within their classes. Ensure that pupil information is shared with staff. • Share with staff the statistics in Chapter 1 of this book about the percentages of the population with various needs. This should help them to see how many of their students will have similar needs.
'I teach a practical subject. Students don't have any difficulties in my subjects.'	• All students will have different individual needs and will experience difficulties in different subjects and activities. • Highlight to staff difficulties that can be created by the physical environment, whatever the subject or topic being taught. • Highlight too that difficulties and differences students face are not limited to reading and writing. Explain other difficulties that can arise which are pertinent in a range of practical subjects as well as academic subjects: understanding and using language, social interaction, group work, memory, organisation, working independently, sensory sensitivities, motor difficulties.
'They can't use (voice-text software/ task boards/ resource x) in their exams or in the real world, so they're not using it in my class. I've got to prepare them for life.'	• Although this argument may have been valid 20 or 30 years ago, it does not reflect the current situation. The reality is that students will have these helpful resources available in future study, employment and their personal lives – we all do, in the form of our mobile phones, computers and laptops. There are also examination access arrangements available to some eligible students (i.e. the use of extra time, a scribe, software or reader) so the sooner they get used to using similar strategies, the better prepared they will be for their examinations. • Many effective strategies and resources are also designed to support students to gain independence and over time to be able to work without the additional resource they once needed. If students are not allowed to use these strategies, they will not be able to build up this level of independence. • Finally, we would not expect adults to do without helpful strategies such as to-do lists, diaries or planning time, so there is no argument for not allowing students to use these.

cont.

Unhelpful attitude	Possible strategies
'I'm not treating one student differently to any other. We need equality and fairness.'	• Equality is not about treating everybody exactly the same; it is about giving individual students the support or resources they need to be able to access education. If you had a student with difficulty walking, you would not deny them a wheelchair because it would be 'treating them differently'. Neurological differences should be treated no differently from physical ones. • The Equality Act of 2010 states that 'reasonable adjustments' need to be made to enable disabled individuals (and that includes those with neurological differences) to be able to access services such as education.
'We coped without that sort of stuff when I was at school.'	• Many of the resources and knowledge at our disposal today were not available a generation or so ago. Adults have generally not rejected using mobiles or the internet because 'we coped without it when I was young' but have embraced them in their personal and professional lives. The world is a different place than it was in the past and it is unhelpful to ignore this. Young people today are growing up with different resources, values and influences than previous generations. They are engaged in an education system and employment landscape which looks very different to their predecessors'. The education system needs to change to reflect the changes in wider society. If it does not, it will not be preparing young people for their futures.
'Conditions such as autism and dyslexia don't really exist. It's just people making a fuss. They just need to get on with it.'	• If conditions like these do not exist, then it is a large proportion of the population who 'just need to get on with it'. Refer again to the statistics in Chapter 1 of this book. • Having outside speakers to talk about their individual experiences can be effective – there may even be staff or parents within the school who would be willing to talk about their own differences. • Explain, using the neurodiversity paradigm, how many of the difficulties come about from unaccepting attitudes and a society/systems designed for one way of being, rather than there being something 'wrong' with the individual.
'I don't have time to meet all these different needs with everything else I have to do.'	• Most of the strategies suggested in this book require no, or very little, additional time. Some of the most effective things that can help are changing attitudes, adapting your communication style and making small tweaks to teaching and learning practices. Mostly it is a case of getting into good habits and routines. You do not need to become an expert in each individual condition; simply change your approach and everyday activities to become more inclusive of a greater range of individuals. • Include meeting the needs of a neurodiverse student population in your general school staff training calendar, rather than making it something 'extra' that staff have to take on board. • 'Drip feed' the approach slowly to staff, encouraging them to make just small changes over a period of time. • If time really is an issue and staff are feeling overwhelmed, consider the bigger picture. Are staff being expected to do too much? What can be done to reduce workloads?

Other staff may be very enthusiastic but simply not know where to start or what to do differently. So what can you do to help to imbed new approaches amongst your staff?

- Traditional staff training sessions during staff meetings or on in-service training (INSET) days can be opportunities to discuss ideas for different areas. Perhaps focus on one area at a time – discussing how to support reading and writing one session, how to adapt communication the next, considering the physical environment after that, for example.

- Bringing in speakers can be an effective way to make these topics more personal and to give a deeper insight into the difficulties that can arise for individuals. There are a number of professional speakers who talk on different topics. Alternatively, there might be members of staff, governors, parents or people within the local community who would be willing to talk about their own experiences of dyslexia, dyspraxia, ADHD or autism, for example. It can also be effective for students themselves to put together a presentation or video aimed at staff about how they experience the world and what would make school life easier for them.

- Host a 'TeachMeet' focusing on inclusion or neurodiversity. At a TeachMeet, teachers and other school staff each take a short slot (usually two to five minutes) to share a resource, strategy or approach with their colleagues. Staff can present or just be enthusiastic audience members. These events are often fun, sociable evenings including refreshments, exhibitions and giveaways. They can also be good opportunities to network with staff from other schools.

- Have a 'bring and share' or 'resource exchange' instead of a traditional staff meeting. Encourage each member of staff to bring one effective resource or strategy that they currently use to share with their colleagues.

- Focus observations and learning walks on inclusive teaching for neurodiversity. Use some of the checklists included in this book to support staff to understand what you are looking for and why those strategies are helpful.

- Provide a drop-in session for staff to turn up with questions and problems they would like to discuss.

- Use staff coaching sessions to focus on meeting the needs of a neurodiverse student population. Peer mentoring can also be effective and can encourage staff to learn from each other and to focus specifically on a topic.

- Provide ready-to-use resources for each member of staff or each classroom.

- Provide useful handouts and lists of strategies for staff to take on board. Display these also on staff notice boards, in each department or in staff bulletins.

- One resourceful SENCO even introduced 'learning in the loo' in her school, displaying a list of effective strategies on the back of each of the cubicle doors in the staff toilets. She changed them each week and found the information reached more staff than simply putting it in an email or giving out another piece of paper.

Teacher/teaching assistant self-evaluation

Support teaching staff to evaluate their current skills and knowledge with this self-evaluation. Collate the results and aim any professional development opportunities at the areas most staff would like support with. There are also individual checklists in previous chapters if you decide you would like to focus on a specific issue in more detail.

Teacher/teaching assistant self-evaluation

	I do not feel confident in this area	Sometimes I do this but not consistently	I mostly do this	I feel confident I do this well
In my subject:				
I know how to support students who are weak readers				
I know how to support students who have difficulty writing				
I communicate instructions and information effectively to students who have difficulty understanding				
I know how to support students who have difficulty using language				
I know how to make the classroom a communication-friendly environment				
I provide helpful resources for students in the classroom and make these accessible to all				
I know how to support students to work independently				
I know how to support memory difficulties				
I teach students how to improve their organisational and planning skills				
I ensure that my classroom does not create sensory overload for students				
I know how I can help to reduce anxieties in the classroom				
I promote acceptance of difference and encourage students to celebrate their individuality				
I support students to celebrate their progress, not just their attainment				

PROMOTING POSITIVE ATTITUDES TOWARDS NEURODIVERSITY

The neurodiversity paradigm is about accepting that neurological difference is part of the natural diversity of being human. It is not about labelling different groups as being 'inferior' or less valuable. It is about making sure everyday school life caters for the neurological diversity of the population and does not inadvertently discriminate against certain groups. So what are the key points in promoting positive attitudes towards these neurological differences?

- Make it clear from the beginning, to both staff and students, that every individual thinks, learns and relates differently to others – and that every way is equally valid. Help students to grow up with this attitude so that they do not see themselves, or other students, as having something 'wrong' with them.

- Encourage all students to accept difference of all types. Ensure that all adults are modelling this way of thinking.

- Do not promote just one way of being as 'acceptable' – for example, an intense emphasis across every aspect of school on the importance of literacy, might lower dyslexics' self-esteem even further, and a culture which focuses only on the importance of team sports might have negative consequences for those who find these difficult. Instead promote a range of values and ensure that everything is put into perspective. Literacy, team sports, etc. are important, but accept that everybody has different strengths and learns differently.

- Support all students to develop self-esteem and self-acceptance. Help students to identify their strengths and to develop strategies to cope with any difficulties.

- Don't allow a difference to become a difficulty. Anticipate a range of needs and plan for these by providing support, understanding and useful resources before they are needed. You do not have to wait until a difficulty is labelled or diagnosed before helping a student. Meet the need, not the label. Students who receive support too late are likely to have experienced repeated failure, low self-esteem and other difficulties, often turning a small difference into a larger problem.

- Avoid stereotypes and prejudices. Consider carefully what messages you are giving out about different needs or disabilities. If you are taking part in awareness days or activities, consider what message is being given and the possible impact on students who identify with that label. A more effective approach could be to promote awareness and understanding of all difference, not just one identified condition.

- Share the school's ethos with parents and encourage them to expect and accept neurological difference. Share useful resources and strategies which can be used in the home environment. Encourage a proactive approach with the focus on developing strengths rather than on weaknesses.

- Challenge any negative attitudes that you encounter amongst students, staff, parents or the community.

POLICIES

Most schools and colleges are full of policies. Perhaps you have a behaviour policy, rewards policy, uniform policy, attendance policy, inclusion policy, homework policy and so on. Generally these policies will have been designed for 'neurotypical' students rather than for the neurodiverse student population in your classrooms. Look at the examples on the next page of how some policies may be interpreted by some 'neurodivergent' students.

WHAT'S A REWARD?

Amelia has an autism spectrum condition. She finds break times difficult as she does not enjoy this unstructured socialising. She ends up feeling left out and isolated, often standing by herself or being with a group of pupils but not feeling relaxed around them. The rewards and sanctions policy at the school states that students who do not complete enough work in lesson time will have to stay inside in the library at break and lunch time to catch up. For Amelia, this does not seem a punishment but a more enjoyable way of spending those social times than outside on the playground.

'NO HANDS UP'

A secondary school realises that it is always the same students who put their hands up every lesson to volunteer answers and that some students are not engaging in lessons. To combat this they bring in a new rule, 'No Hands Up'. Students are not to put their hand up but should be prepared to give answers whenever the teacher asks them. Elliot wants to ask for help in the lesson but he remembers that there is a 'No Hands Up' policy so continues to struggle with the work, not understanding what he is doing. Jessica experiences considerable anxiety about speaking in front of her peers and she begins to try to avoid attending as many lessons as possible.

TOP TIP! Consider all of the 'rules', policies and expectations that you have in place. Are they all enforced and do they make sense? If not, maybe you no longer need the 'rule'. Getting rid of it will eliminate confusion for students. Make sure rules, rewards and sanctions are applied consistently.

When creating or updating policies, there are a number of points to take into consideration:

Does the policy in any way discriminate against neurodivergent students? If so, how are we going to amend it? How are we going to respond to exceptions?

Disability is considered a protected characteristic under the Equality Act (2010). A disability is defined in section six of the Equality Act as *'a physical or mental impairment that has a substantial and long-term adverse effect on a person's ability to carry out normal day-to-day activities'*. For the purposes of this act conditions such as dyslexia, dyspraxia, autism, ADHD and developmental language disorder are all classed as 'mental impairments'. This means that it is unlawful for educational establishments to treat students with these conditions less favourably than other students. The types of discrimination which are prohibited by the Equality Act include discrimination arising from a disability, direct and indirect discrimination, failure to make reasonable adjustments, victimisation and harassment.

Schools and colleges have a duty to make 'reasonable adjustments' to make sure that students are not discriminated against. A 'reasonable adjustment' might need to be made to policies and practices, the physical environment or an auxiliary aid in order to ensure that students are not put at a substantial disadvantage.

Remember that the duty to make reasonable adjustments in education is *anticipatory*. This means schools must consider in advance what they need to do to make sure all students can access and participate in the education and other benefits, facilities and services they provide.

TOP TIP! Remember not to be too fixed on official 'labels' or 'diagnoses'. Just because a student does not have a label does not mean you should not put in place what that student needs. It may be that some students are on a lengthy waiting list for an assessment or some may have chosen not to pursue a formal diagnosis, seeing their differences as just a different way of being.

What message is this policy giving to staff, parents and students?

Think about the message each of your policies is giving out to staff, parents and pupils. What is each policy saying about what the school values or does not value? How could these things make some neurodivergent individuals feel?

Does the way a policy is implemented have a negative impact on neurodivergent students? If so, how can we change it?

Remember that, sometimes, a policy or 'rule' might not in itself be discriminatory, but the way it is implemented can make a big difference. Take, for example, a school's healthy eating policy. Imagine a school which takes this to the extreme – not only promoting healthy eating but banning any sort of unhealthy snack, reinforcing 'unhealthy' foods at every opportunity. Now imagine a student in this school with diabetes who needs a sugary snack in order to maintain her blood sugar levels. Knowing the school policy on this which has been reiterated to her and her friends, this student may feel less accepting of her diabetes. She might begin to feel embarrassed about her needs because of the messages that have been given out to other students. The same principle applies for individual needs relating to neurodiversity.

WHERE ARE YOU NOW?

Having read the previous chapters you will have begun to gain an insight into some of the difficulties for a neurodiverse student population in mainstream schools and some of the things that can be done to support these differences and difficulties. You might want to begin by considering your school, department or area of responsibility currently. Where would you rate yourself?

★ *Where are you now?*

	We do not yet do this well	We do this sometimes/ in some cases but not consistently	Generally we do this, but could make some improve-ments	We always do this well
Teachers know how to communicate effectively to students who are having difficulty understanding or using language				
Non-teaching staff know how to communicate effectively to students who have difficulty understanding or using language				
Written information around the school is relevant, up to date and accessible to all				
Classrooms are kept clean, tidy and uncluttered				
Displays in classrooms and corridors are relevant, tidy and uncluttered				
Corridors and shared spaces are kept tidy and are easy to navigate				
Background noise and visual distractions are eliminated wherever possible				
Quiet areas are available for all students to use when they need to				
There are a range of options for students at social times during the day				
Students who find reading and writing difficult are supported across the curriculum and are allowed to demonstrate their knowledge in different ways				
Written materials are clearly presented and accessible				

cont.

	We do not yet do this well	We do this sometimes/ in some cases but not consistently	Generally we do this, but could make some improve- ments	We always do this well
Group work is clearly managed and social communication differences are taken into account				
Clear written instructions are given for homework tasks and students are provided with useful resources				
A variety of helpful resources is available in the classroom for all students to use				
We communicate with parents effectively and utilise their knowledge and expertise				
Consistent routines are in place across the school day and across different subject areas				
Staff have clear and consistent expectations				
Students feel confident to ask for help and to use helpful resources and equipment				
All adults model positive attitudes and acceptance of difference				
The ethos is that it is 'normal to be different' and that every individual will have different needs, likes and preferences				
Students are supported to work with increasing independence				

Staff anticipate that there will be a range of needs in every class and will plan for these in advance							
Students know where to get support in different areas							
Student views are taken into account and acted upon							
Views are collected from a wide spectrum of the student population							
Students are not labelled, marginalised or isolated because of their diagnosis or needs							
Students are encouraged to identify their strengths and to work with their individuality							
We recognise and celebrate progress and achievement of all types							
Policies are designed not to discriminate against or marginalise those who learn, think or relate to others differently							
What evidence do you have to support the areas that you do well?							
Which areas have you identified for further development?							

ACTION PLANNING

Using your discussions from the previous activity, make an action plan for your school, department or area of responsibility.

★ *Action plan*

Areas for development	Steps we will take	Who is responsible	Time frame

KEY POINTS

- A whole school approach is only as successful as the people leading it and the consistency with which it is applied.

- It is important that all staff working within the school are given the same messages about neurodiversity and the approach that your setting takes.

- Often, implementing more positive practices and a neurodiverse-friendly ethos in your school is about changing attitudes. Staff may initially be resistant to changing or challenging long-held beliefs. Try to be creative in how you introduce and implement new ideas.

- Supporting neurodiversity is not only about what is going on in the classroom. The policies that are in place can also contribute to the wellbeing and acceptance of neurodivergent students. Consider if your school policies may discriminate against certain groups of students.

ABBREVIATIONS

A list of abbreviations relating to special educational needs, inclusion and neurodiversity.

ADD	Attention deficit disorder
ADHD	Attention deficit hyperactivity disorder
AEN	Additional educational needs
AENCO	Additional educational needs co-ordinator
ALN	Additional learning needs
ALNCO	Additional learning needs co-ordinator (Wales)
ASC	Autism spectrum condition
ASD	Autism spectrum disorder
ASN	Additional support needs (Scotland)
BDA	British Dyslexia Association
BSL	British Sign Language
CAMHS	Child and adolescent mental health service
COP	Code of Practice
DCD	Developmental co-ordination disorder
DLD	Developmental language disorder
EAL	English as an Additional Language
EHCP	Education, health and care plan
EP	Educational psychologist
HI	Hearing impairment

HLTA	Higher level teaching assistant
IEP	Individual Education Plan
IPM	Individual Provision Map
LSA	Learning support assistant
LD	Learning difficulty
MLD	Moderate learning difficulties
MSI	Multi-sensory impairment
OCD	Obsessive compulsive disorder
ODD	Oppositional defiance disorder
OT	Occupational therapist
PD	Physical disabilities
PDA	Pathological demand avoidance
PDD-NOS	Pervasive developmental disorder – not otherwise specified
PMLD	Profound and multiple learning difficulties
PT	Physiotherapist
SaLT	Speech and language therapist
SEMH	Social, emotional and mental health needs
SEN	Special educational needs
SENCO	Special educational needs co-ordinator (England)
SEND	Special educational needs and disability
SLCN	Speech, language and communication needs
SLI	Specific language impairment
SLD	Severe learning difficulties
SpLD	Specific learning difficulty
TA	Teaching assistant
VI	Visual impairment

FURTHER RESOURCES

ADHD

ADHD Foundation
www.adhdfoundation.org.uk

ADHD Kids
http://adhdkids.org.uk

**ADDISS (National Attention Deficit Disorder
Information and Support Service)**
www.addiss.co.uk

O'Regan, F. (2007) *ADHD*, 2nd edn. London: Continuum.

AUTISM

Ambitious about Autism
www.ambitiousaboutautism.org.uk

Autism Education Trust (AET)
www.autismeducationtrust.org.uk

Autism New Zealand
www.autismnz.org.nz

Autism Canada
https://autismscanada.org

Autism Spectrum Australia
https://www.autismspectrum.org.au

Autism West Midlands
www.autismwestmidlands.org.uk

National Autistic Society (NAS)
www.autism.org.uk

The Den
www.theden.me

US Autism & Asperger Association
www.usautism.org

Attwood, T. (2007) *The Complete Guide to Asperger's Syndrome.* London: Jessica Kingsley Publishers.

DYSCALCULIA

British Dyslexia Association
www.bdadyslexia.org.uk/dyslexic/dyscalculia

Bird, R. (2017) *The Dyscalculia Toolkit,* 3rd edn. London: Sage.

DYSLEXIA

American Dyslexia Association
www.american-dyslexia-association.com

Australian Dyslexia Association
http://dyslexiaassociation.org.au

British Dyslexia Association (BDA)
www.bdadyslexia.org.uk

Canadian Dyslexia Association
www.dyslexiaassociation.ca

Dyslexia Action
www.dyslexiaaction.org.uk

Helen Arkell Dyslexia Association
www.arkellcentre.org.uk

Irlen Institute
www.irlen.com

National Literacy Trust
www.literacytrust.org.uk

PATOSS
www.patoss-dyslexia.org

Reid, G. (2009) *Dyslexia: A Practitioner's Guide,* 4th edn. London: Wiley.

Rooke, M. (2015) *Creative, Successful, Dyslexic.* London: Jessica Kingsley Publishers.

DYSPRAXIA

Dyspraxia Foundation
www.dyspraxiafoundation.org.uk

Dyspraxia Foundation USA
www.dyspraxiausa.org

MENTAL HEALTH NEEDS

Childline
www.childline.org

HeadMeds (information aimed at young people about medication)
www.headmeds.org

Minded (free online training modules for both professionals and parents in all aspects of mental and emotional wellbeing)
www.minded.org

Mind
www.mind.org.uk

OCD Action
www.ocdaction.org.uk

Young Minds
www.youngminds.org.uk

PATHOLOGICAL DEMAND AVOIDANCE

PDA Society
www.pdasociety.org.uk

SPECIAL EDUCATIONAL NEEDS AND INCLUSION

MENCAP
www.mencap.org.uk

NASEN (National Association for Special Educational Needs)
www.nasen.org.uk

SCOPE
www.scope.org.uk

SEND gateway
www.sendgateway.org.uk

SPEECH, LANGUAGE AND COMMUNICATION NEEDS

Afasic
www.afasic.org.uk

British Stammering Association
www.stammering.org

Communication Trust
www.thecommunicationtrust.org.uk

I CAN
www.ican.org.uk

Language for Learning
www.languageforlearning.co.uk

NAPLIC (National Association of Professionals Concerned with Language Impairment in Children)
www.naplic.org.uk

SMIRA (Selective Mutism Information and Research Association)
www.selectivemutism.co.uk

REFERENCES

Afasic (2016) *GlossAry: Developmental Language Disorder (Previously Specific Language Impairment)*. Afasic: London. Accessed on 11/12/2017 at www.afasic.org.uk/download/1.

Allen, J. (2003) 'Productive pedagogies and the challenge of inclusion.' *British Journal of Special Education 30*, 4, 175–179.

Attwood, T. (2007) *The Complete Guide to Asperger's Syndrome*. London: Jessica Kingsley Publishers.

BDA (British Dyslexia Association) (n.d.) 'About the British Dyslexia Association.' Accessed on 11/12/2017 at www.bdadyslexia.org.uk/about.

BDA (2015) 'Dyscalculia.' Accessed on 19/12/2017 at www.bdadyslexia.org.uk/dyslexic/dyscalculia.

BDA (British Dyslexia Association) (2017) 'Dyslexia Style Guide.' Accessed on 11/12/2017 at www.bdadyslexia.org.uk/common/ckeditor/filemanager/userfiles/About_Us/policies/Dyslexia_Style_Guide.pdf.

Communication Trust (2014) 'Children and Young People's Speech, Language and Communication Needs – An Introduction for Health Audiences.' Accessed on 11/12/2017 at www.thecommunicationtrust.org.uk/media/266719/the_communication_council_slcn_briefing_for_health_audiences-_september_2014.pdf.

Department for Education (2015) *Special Educational Needs and Disability Code of Practice: 0 to 25 years: Statutory Guidance for Organisations Which Work with and Support Children and Young People Who Have Special Educational Needs or Disabilities*. London: Department for Education/Department for Health. Accessed on 19/12/2017 at www.gov.uk/government/uploads/system/uploads/attachment_data/file/398815/SEND_Code_of_Practice_January_2015.pdf.

Dray, M., Campbell, M. A. and Gilmore, L. A. (2006) 'Why are girls with ADHD invisible?' *Connections 23*, 2, 2–7. Queensland: Queensland Guidance and Counselling Association.

Dweck, C. (2006) *Mindset: The Psychology of Success*. New York: Ballantine Books.

Dyspraxia Foundation (2015) 'About Dyspraxia.' Accessed on 11/12/2017 at http://dyspraxiafoundation.org.uk/about-dyspraxia.

Elder Robison, J. (2015) 'Neurodiversity: What Does It Mean for 2015?' Accessed on 11/12/2017 at www.psychologytoday.com/blog/my-life-aspergers/201503/neurodiversity-what-does-it-mean-2015.

Frederickson, N. and Cline, T. (2002) *Special Educational Needs, Inclusion and Diversity*. Buckingham: Oxford University Press.

Frederickson, N. and Cline, T. (2009) *Special Educational Needs, Inclusion and Diversity*, 2nd edn. Maidenhead: Oxford University Press.

Goering, S. (2010) 'Revisiting the relevance of the social model of disability.' *American Journal of Bioethics 10*, 1, 54–55.

Government Equalities Office and Equality and Human Rights Commission (2010) 'Equality Act 2010.' Accessed on 09/03/2018 at www.legislation.gov.uk/ukpga/2010/15/contents.

Grant, D. (2017) *That's the Way I Think: Dyslexia, Dyspraxia, ADHD and Dyscalculia Explained*, 3rd edn. Abingdon: David Fulton.

Herbert, S. (2011) *The Inclusion Toolkit.* London: Sage.

Hodkinson, A. (2016) *Key Issues in Special Educational Needs and Inclusion*, 2nd edn. London: Sage.

Honeybourne, V. (2016) *Educating and Supporting Girls with Asperger's and Autism.* London: Sage.

Hudson, D. (2016) *Specific Learning Difficulties: What Teachers Need to Know.* London: Jessica Kingsley Publishers.

Johnstone, D. (2001) *An Introduction to Disability Studies*, 2nd edn. London: David Fulton.

Kidd, D. and Castano, E. (2013) 'Reading literary fiction improves theory of mind.' *Science 342*, 6156, 117–132.

Kim, J. A., Szatmari, P., Bryson, S., Streiner, D. L. and Wilson, F. (2000) 'The prevalence of anxiety and mood problems among children with autism and Asperger syndrome.' *Autism: The International Journal of Research and Practice 4*, 2, 117–132.

Kutscher, M. L. (2016) *Digital Kids: How to Balance Screen Time and Why It Matters.* London: Jessica Kingsley Publishers.

Law, J., McBean, K. and Rush, R. (2011) 'Communication skills in a population of primary school-aged children raised in an area of pronounced social disadvantage.' *International Journal of Language & Communication Disorders 46*, 6, 657–664.

Missiuna, C., Gaines, R., Soucie, H. and McLean, J. (2006) 'Parental questions about developmental co-ordination disorder: A synopsis of current evidence.' *Paediatric Child Health 11*, 8, 507–512.

Myttas, N. (2009) 'Gender disparities: Adolescent girls with ADHD.' *ADHD in Practice 1*, 4, 8–11.

NASS (National Association of Independent Schools and Non-Maintained Special Schools) (2015) 'Making Sense of Mental Health.' Accessed on 11/12/2017 at https://www.nasschools.org/wp-content/uploads/sites/9/public/Making-Sense-of-Mental-Health.pdf.

National Autistic Society (2016) 'What Is Autism?' Accessed on 11/12/2017 at www.autism.org.uk/about/what-is/asd.aspx.

National Autistic Society (2017) 'Autism Facts and History.' Accessed on 11/12/2017 at www.autism.org.uk/about/what-is/myths-facts-stats.aspx.

National Health Service (2016a) 'Developmental Co-Ordination Disorder (Dyspraxia) in Children.' Accessed on 11/12/2017 at www.nhs.uk/conditions/Dyspraxia-(childhood)/Pages/Introduction.aspx.

National Health Service (2016b) 'Attention Deficit Hyperactivity Disorder: ADHD.' Accessed on 11/12/2017 at www.nhs.uk/conditions/attention-deficit-hyperactivity-disorder/Pages/Introduction.aspx.

Oliver, M. (1990) *The Politics of Disablement.* Basingstoke: Macmillan.

Oliver, M. (2013) 'The social model of disability: Thirty years on.' *Disability and Society 28,* 7, 1024–1026.

Oliver, M. and Barnes, C. (1998) *Disabled People and Social Policy: From Exclusion to Inclusion.* Harlow: Addison Wesley Longman.

O'Regan, F. J. (2007) *ADHD*, 2nd edn. London: Continuum.

Reid, G. (2013) *Dyslexia and Inclusion: Classroom Approaches for Assessment, Teaching and Learning.* Abingdon: Routledge.

Roberts, M. (2015) 'Write your thoughts in a diary.' *Psychologies Magazine,* August, 39.

Rose Report (2009) 'Identifying and teaching children and young people with dyslexia and reading difficulties.' Accessed on 19/12/2017 at www.thedyslexia-spldtrust.org.uk/media/downloads/inline/the-rose-report.1294933674.pdf.

Seligman, M. (2002) *Authentic Happiness.* New York: Free Press.

Siegel, L. S. and Smythe, I. S. (2005) 'Reflections on research on reading disability with special attention to gender issues.' *Journal of Learning Disabilities 38,* 5, 473–477.

Skidmore, D. (1996) 'Towards an integrated theoretical framework for research in special educational needs.' *European Journal of Special Educational Needs Education 11,* 1, 33–42.

Slorach, R. (2016) *A Very Capitalist Condition: A History and Politics of Disability.* London: Bookmarks Publications.

Stahl, R. J. (1994) *Using Think Time and Wait Time Skilfully in the Classroom.* Bloomington, IN: ERIC Clearinghouse for social science education. Accessed on 11/12/2017 at www.ericdigests.org/1995-1/think.htm.

Swain, J. and French, S. (2000) 'Towards an affirmation model of disability.' *Disability and Society 15,* 4, 569–582.

Swain, J. and French, S. (2004) 'Whose Tragedy?: Towards a Personal Non-Tragedy View of Disability.' In J. Swain, S. French, C. Barnes and C. Thomas (eds) *Disabling Barriers – Enabling Environments.* London: Sage.

Terzi, L. (2005) 'Beyond the dilemma of difference: The capability approach to disability and special educational needs.' *Journal of Philosophy in Education 19,* 3, 443–459.

Walker, N. (2014) 'Neurodiversity: Some basic terms and definitions.' Neurocosmopolitanism Blog. Accessed on 11/12/2017 at http://neurocosmopolitanism.com/neurodiversity-some-basic-terms-definitions.

INDEX